Most Wanted

Also by Mike Fitzgerald Jr.

Earnie Shavers: Welcome to the Big Time with Earnie Shavers and Marshall Terrill

Going the Distance: The Ken Norton Story with Ken Norton and Marshall Terrill

Tale of the Gator: The Story of Craig Bodzianowski, the Boxer Who Wouldn't Stay Down with Craig Bodzianowski

Also by David L. Hudson Jr.

The Fourteenth Amendment: Equal Protection Under the Law

The Bill of Rights: The First Ten Amendments of the Constitution

The First Amendment in Schools with Charles Haynes, Sam Chaltain, John Ferguson, and Oliver Thomas

Boxing's Most Wanted

The Top 10 Book of Champs, Chumps, and Punch-Drunk Palookas

David L. Hudson Jr. and Mike H. Fitzgerald Jr.

Brassey's, Inc.

WASHINGTON, D.C.

Library of Congress Cataloging-in-Publication Data

Hudson, David (David L.), 1969–
  Boxing's most wanted : the top 10 book of
champs, chumps, and punch-drunk palookas /
David L. Hudson, Jr. and Mike H. Fitzgerald, Jr.—
1st ed.
       p.   cm.
  Includes bibliographical references and index.
  ISBN 1-57488-714-9 (alk. paper)
  1. Boxing—Anecdotes.   I. Fitzgerald,
Mike H.   II. Title

GV1135.H83   2003
796.83—dc22   2003024406

Printed in Canada on acid-free paper that meets the
American National Standards Institute Z39-48 Standard.

Brassey's, Inc.
22841 Quicksilver Drive
Dulles, Virginia 20166

First Edition

10   9   8   7   6   5   4   3   2   1

To Flattop and Charles Welfel
—David L. Hudson Jr.

To my son, Ross, and my friend Bob Lynch—Bob,
thanks for all the great boxing-related experiences
you brought to Madison. I miss Monday nights at
the local watering hole.
—Mike H. Fitzgerald Jr.

Contents

List of Photographs   xiii

Boxing Firsts   1
Famous boxing firsts

Undefeated Fighters   6
I never lost a pro bout

I Only Lost Once   11
Fighters with just one loss

Great Trilogies   16
Three times to do battle

Great Upsets in Heavyweight Title Bouts   21
Longshots that captured the crown

Come-from-Behind Kayoes   27
"The opera ain't over till the fat lady sings" (or the final bell rings)

Most Title Defenses   35
Hanging on to my title

Greatest Punchers   39
They packed a wallop

Youngest Champions   44
I won the title at an early age

No Time to Waste for World Title   48
Fighters who won the title with few fights

Great Fighters Who Never Fought for a Belt   53
I never got my title shot

Worst Heavyweight Challengers   59
I didn't earn my title shot

Hapless Heavyweights   65
Big guys born to lose in the ring

The Journeyman/Survivors   69
Lasting till the final bell

Controversial Decisions   74
When the wrong guy wins

Dirty Fighters   82
Fouling is part of my game

Prison Boxers   86
Learning to box in the big house

Cop Boxers   92
On the right side of the law

Worst Ring Tragedies   98
Death in the ring

Death Behind the Wheel   107
Boxers who died in automobile accidents

"Suicide Solution"   112
Boxers and boxing personalities who killed
themselves

Like Father, Like Son   **117**
Boxing in the bloodlines

Boxing Brothers   **123**
Fighting siblings in the ring

She Can Fight, Too   **129**
Female fighters with famous male-relative boxers

Boxers and Football   **133**
Boxers who loved the gridiron

Boxing B-Ballers   **138**
Fighters with hoop dreams

Boxing and Kickboxing   **143**
Can't fight with your legs anymore

Tough Man to Real Pro   **149**
From the minor leagues to the real thing

Boxer vs. Wrestler   **154**
When boxing and sports entertainment shared the
squared circle

Highly Educated Boxers   **161**
As much brains as brawn

Boxers/Referees   **165**
From a pugilist to the third man in the ring

Boxing Musicians   **170**
Boxers with a love of music

Heavyweights in Hollywood   **175**
Big guys who landed on the screen

Top Boxing Movies   **179**
The best of cinema and pugilism

**Real Boxing Personalities in the Reel *Rocky*
Saga**　　　183
Appearing with Sylvester Stallone

Boxing Figures in the Movie *Ali*　　　187
On the screen with Will Smith and Jamie Foxx

Named by Ali　　　190
Ali's nicknames for his opponents

Famous Boxing Quotes　　　195
Comments with a lasting legacy

Boxers' Real Names　　　201
I changed my name

Here's Your "Sugar" Fix　　　205
Fighters sweet as sugar

Just Call Me "Kid"　　　209
Great fighters named "Kid"

Nonagenarians　　　213
I lived to the age of ninety and beyond

Female Firsts　　　217
On the distaff side

Black Pioneers　　　221
Paving the way for the next generation

Puerto Rican Greats　　　226
Great fighters from the island

Colombian Champions　　　232
Champions from the South American country

Born in Georgia　　　236
Fighters from the "Peach State"

Homegrown Heroes   **240**
 Fighting in my own backyard

Debut Debacles   **245**
 I lost my first pro fight

Ring Weirdness   **251**
 Strange stuff in the ring

Bibliography   **257**

Index   **261**

About the Authors   **271**

List of Photographs

Rickey Womack	10
David Tua	33
Donnie Penelton	72
Michael Bennett	90
Tunney Hunsaker	96
Chris Byrd	120
Laila Ali	130
Mike Nevitt	146
John Yost	151
Mike Rodgers	174
Eric Morel	230
Matt Vanda	243

Boxing Firsts

Though its roots come from ancient Greece and Rome, modern-day boxing arose in eighteenth-century England. Bare knuckle fighters brawled for glory and prize belts. Eventually, the sport would develop a set of rules, including those drafted by John Graham Chambers and sponsored by the Marquis of Queensberry in 1867. These rules established three-minute rounds separated by one-minute rest periods. The sport has seen many pioneers in its colorful history. The following is a list of prominent boxing firsts.

1. JAMES FIGG

James Figg was a walking who's who of boxing firsts. He was England's first bare knuckle champion, the first man to open a boxing stadium, and the first man to actively promote the sport. Figg became the first recognized English champion in 1719, a status cemented by his defeat of Timothy Buck in 1720 in what historians consider the first championship fight in Great Britain. Figg remained undefeated and officially retired in 1734. He established the first boxing stadium in 1719, called Figg's Amphitheatre, in London. In addition to his boxing abilities, Figg was an expert fencer.

2. JACK BROUGHTON

Called the "Father of Boxing," boxer Jack Broughton of England devised the first set of boxing rules in 1743, called "Broughton's Rules." He drafted the rules two years after one of his opponents, George Stevenson, died from blows in their ring encounter. The rules prohibited hitting an opponent while he was on the ground. They also allowed a boxer thirty seconds to get to his feet after being knocked down. In 1747, Broughton introduced the first set of boxing gloves, or "mufflers." Broughton was a great fighter who defeated George Taylor in 1738 to become the recognized heavyweight champion. He retired after losing to Jack Slack in 1750. He later served as a Yeoman of the Guard at the Tower of London and was buried in Westminster Abbey.

3. TOM CRIBB

Tom Cribb was the first boxing champion to receive a belt as a prize for his ring accomplishments. In December 1810, King George III, the same king whom the American colonists defied in the Declaration of Independence, presented Cribb a belt after he defeated Tom Molineaux, a former American slave. Cribb reigned as bare knuckle champion of England from 1809 until 1822. He defeated Hall of Famers Jem Belcher and Bill Richmond in addition to Molineaux.

4. BOB FITZSIMMONS

Robert James Fitzsimmons, called "Ruby Robert," was the first man to win world titles in three separate weight classes. He won the middleweight title in 1891 by defeating Jack Dempsey ("the Nonpareil") in the thirteenth round. In 1897, Fitzsimmons upset James J. Corbett to win the heavyweight championship. After losing his heavyweight title to James J. Jeffries in 1899, Fitzsimmons next won the world light heavyweight title with a twenty-round decision over George Gardner.

5. AL McCOY

Al McCoy was the first southpaw to win a world boxing championship when he stopped George Chip in the first round in April 1914. McCoy's father, a poultry farmer from New Jersey, actually bet against his own nineteen-year-old son in the bout. However, McCoy landed a big left hook in the opening round to capture the belt. He held the title until suffering a kayo loss to Mike O'Dowd in 1917. McCoy's trainer was the legendary Charley Goodman, best known for guiding Rocky Marciano to the heavyweight title.

6. DANIEL MENDOZA

Daniel Mendoza was the first Jewish fighter to win a boxing title when he became England's heavyweight champion in 1794. Born in London's East End, Mendoza became a true rags-to-riches story. Although he weighed only 160 pounds, Mendoza used his superior boxing skills to defeat much larger opponents. He held the title until suffering a ninth-round knockout at the hands of John Jackson. Mendoza was considered to be one of the most scientific boxers in the history of the sport.

7. TED "KID" LEWIS

Ted "Kid" Lewis, a two-time world welterweight champion, was the first fighter to regularly wear a mouthpiece in the boxing ring. The mouthpiece, designed by British dentist Jack Markes, was a controversial topic in the early 1920s. For example, Lewis's arch rival, Jack Britton, protested that Lewis should not be allowed to wear the mouthpiece. Similarly, the camp of Georges Carpentier objected strenuously to Lewis wearing the mouthpiece for their May 1922 match for the world light heavyweight title. In 1928, Lewis walked out of the ring from his match with Charley Belanger after the referee repeatedly ordered him to remove his mouthpiece.

8. JACK DEMPSEY–GEORGES CARPENTIER

The 1922 showdown between heavyweight champion Jack Dempsey and light heavyweight champion Georges Carpentier was the first fight to gross more than $1 million in gate earnings. The bout, which was held at Boyle's Thirty Acres in Jersey City, New Jersey, saw more than eighty thousand people pay nearly $1.8 million to watch the fight billed as "The Fight of the Century." Promoter George "Tex" Rickard was responsible for the record-setting event. Carpentier stunned Dempsey in the second round, but the heavier Dempsey quickly rebounded to win by kayo in the fourth.

9. SUGAR RAY ROBINSON

Sugar Ray Robinson, the boxer whom most boxing historians rank as the pound-for-pound all-time greatest, was the first man to win a world title in the same division five times. Robinson captured the world middleweight title in 1951 (twice), 1955, 1957, and 1958. Robinson defeated Jake LaMotta in 1951 to win the title the first time, Randy Turpin later in 1951 to regain the title, Carl Olsen in 1955, Gene Fullmer in 1957, and

Carmen Basilio in 1958. Before he moved to middle-weight, Robinson was virtually unbeatable in the wel-terweight division. He won his first forty pro bouts before losing by decision to Jake LaMotta. After that defeat, Robinson would not lose another fight for eight years.

10. JOE FRAZIER

"Smokin" Joe Frazier became the first man to win an Olympic gold medal and a professional world title in the heavyweight division. In 1964, Frazier won the gold medal in Tokyo by defeating West Germany's Hans Huber. Six years later, in 1970, Frazier won the world heavyweight title by stopping Jimmy Ellis in the fifth round. Floyd Patterson and Muhammad Ali also won Olympic gold medals and world heavyweight titles. However, Patterson won his gold medal at middle-weight, and Ali (then Cassius Clay) won his gold medal at light heavyweight.

Undefeated Fighters

V ery few fighters have ever finished a career without a loss, particularly today when all bouts that go the distance go to the scorecards. In the early days, many bouts that went the distance were called "no-decisions," in which neither fighter officially won or lost. Most fighters—even great fighters—lose a few times in their career. But these fighters did not.

1. ROCKY MARCIANO

"The Brockton Blockbuster's" greatest claim to fame is his 49–0 record, a feat unmatched in heavyweight history. For this reason alone, many rate Marciano among the very elite in history. In many fights, Marciano finished off the opposition with his famous right hand that he called the "Suzie-Q." Marciano also possessed an indomitable will to win and an incredible ability to absorb punishment. Several times in his career, he fell behind in the early rounds only to steamroll his opponent in the later rounds. In his first bout with Jersey Joe Walcott to win the world title, Marciano—trailing on the scorecards—landed a single right hand that kayoed his worthy foe.

2. JACK MCAULIFFE

Jack McAuliffe, called the "Napoleon of the Prize Ring," reigned as world lightweight champion from 1886 to 1894. He retired with a record of 30–0–5 with one no-decision. Born in Ireland, McAuliffe moved to the States with his family when he was a boy. McAuliffe fought in a time when there was no twelve-round limit on championship bouts. In one of his more famous bouts, he fought a seventy-four-round draw with British champion Jem Carney.

3. JIMMY BARRY

Called the "Little Tiger," Jimmy Barry stood only 5'2" and weighed approximately one hundred pounds. But he was a master boxer with power in his fists. He fought seventy bouts from 1891 to 1899, finishing with a record of 59–0–9 with two no-contests. In perhaps his most famous bout, Barry kayoed British fighter Walter Croot in the twentieth round in London. Croot hit his head on an unpadded wooden floor and died. Barry was charged with manslaughter, but the charges were dropped. Barry was never the same fighter after the Croot fight.

4. LAZLO PAPP

Hungary's Lazlo Papp won three Olympic gold medals—in 1948, 1952, and 1956. He turned pro in 1957 at the age of thirty-one and never lost a pro fight. He retired in 1964 with a record of 27–0–2. His two draws were to a French fighter in Paris and an Italian fighter in Milan. Unfortunately, politics in his Communist country of Hungary forced him to retire without receiving a shot at the world title. He continued to coach the Hungarian amateur boxing team for many years.

5. RICARDO LOPEZ

Mexico's Ricardo "Finito" Lopez dominated boxing's lightest weight division for nearly a decade, earning accolades as one of the best boxers of his era. Lopez had it all: defense, footwork, stamina, and power. He won his first world title, the WBC strawweight title, in October 1990 and defended it twenty times through the end of the decade. He defeated Rosendo Alvarez in a twelve-round split decision to add the WBA crown in perhaps his toughest fight ever. The only mark on his record was a technical draw to Alvarez caused by an accidental head butt. He announced his retirement in November 2002, finishing with a record of 51–0–1.

6. TERRY MARSH

England's Terry Marsh fought professionally from 1981 to 1987. He captured the British and European light welterweight titles. Then, in March 1987, Marsh defeated Joe Manley to win the IBF light welterweight championship. He defended his title against Japan's Akio Kameda in July 1987 and then retired with a record of 26–0–1. His only blemish was an eight-round draw in his seventh pro fight.

7. JI-WON KIM

Korea's Ji-Won Kim began his career with five wins and two draws. Then he won his remaining eleven fights, including the IBF super bantamweight championship in 1985, which he successfully defended five times. In his last two defenses he won via first- and second-round knockouts. He finished his career with a record of 16–0–2.

8. PICHIT SITBANGPRACHAN

Thailand's Pichit Sitbangprachan fought in the lower weight classes from 1990 to 2000. He won the IBF world flyweight title in 1992 with a third round kayo over Rodolfo Blanco. He held the title until his retirement in 1994. Sitbangprachan came out of retirement for one fight in 1996 and two fights in 2000. His record was 23–0 with 17 knockouts. He never fought outside his home country of Thailand.

9. JEMAL HINTON

Jemal Hinton could have won a world title but retired after winning his first sixteen bouts before he ever got the chance. Hinton showed great promise, winning the WBC Continental Americas super bantamweight title with a victory over Robert Shannon in 1989. He defended his title twice. He retired in 1992 as a top-ten fighter, saying he wanted to focus on his Muslim faith.

10. RICKEY WOMACK

It would be hard to find a sadder story than that of Rickey Womack. A decorated amateur, Womack defeated Evander Holyfield three times in the amateurs. He turned pro in 1984 and won his first ten fights. However, he was convicted of attempted murder and armed robbery and served sixteen years in prison. Amazingly, he returned to the ring at age thirty-nine and won four straight bouts. However, Womack could not beat his personal demons and committed suicide in January 2002.

Max Ortiz/Dr. Stuart Kirshenbaum

Rickey Womack started with promise, defeating Evander Holyfield three times in the amateur ranks. His career was derailed by a conviction for attempted murder and ended by a suicide.

I Only Lost Once

Only a very few boxers have ever reached the highest levels of the sport without losing a bout. Rocky Marciano (49–0) remains the only heavyweight champion to ever retire (for good) unbeaten. In fact, most boxers that reach the highest levels of the sport lose multiple bouts. For instance, Hall of Famer Fritzie Zivic, a welterweight champion, lost sixty-four bouts.

A few championship-level fighters lost only one fight in their pro career. Currently, the talented Roy Jones Jr. has only one loss on his record—a disqualification in his first fight with Montell Griffin, because he hit Griffin when he was down. Another fighter of recent vintage, former heavyweight champion Riddick Bowe, lost only once during his career. The following fighters all lost only one bout in their championship-level careers.

1. GENE TUNNEY

Gene Tunney, known as the "Fighting Marine," never achieved the public recognition that he deserved because he twice defeated the popular slugger Jack Dempsey. Tunney didn't capture public adulation in part because he was more of a scientific boxer than a brawler like Dempsey. Tunney began his career as a light heavyweight. In 1922, he lost a fifteen-round decision to Hall of Famer Harry Greb for the U.S. light heavyweight championship. Tunney avenged the loss the next year with a vicious body attack. He beat Dempsey in 1926 to win the world heavyweight title. In 1927, he won the rematch with Dempsey in the fight known for the "Long Count." Tunney defended his title one more time and then retired with a record of 61–1–1.

2. MICHAEL SPINKS

Michael Spinks dominated the light heavyweight division from 1981 to 1985, dispatching every contender placed in front of him. He felled many of his foes with his classic right cross, called the "Spinks Jinx." In 1985, Spinks shocked the boxing world by defeating unbeaten heavyweight champion Larry Holmes to win the title. He retired after his only loss, a 1988 one-round drubbing at the hands of Mike Tyson.

3. SALVADOR SANCHEZ

Salvador Sanchez accomplished much in his twenty-three years before a fatal car crash. He won the world featherweight title in 1980 with a convincing win over popular champion Danny "Little Red" Lopez and successfully defended his title nine times. At his death, the champion was 44–1–1. His only loss was a twelve-round decision to fellow Mexican Antonio Becerra in 1977 for the Mexican bantamweight championship.

4. AARON PRYOR

Aaron "The Hawk" Pryor reminded many of a modern-day version of Henry Armstrong, with his nonstop, action-packed punching style. Pryor simply over-whelmed opponents with the volume of his punches. He defeated fellow Hall of Famer Antonio Cervantes in 1980 to capture the WBA junior welterweight title. He earned his place in history with two wins over the great Alexis Arguello in classic slugfests. Derailed by drug use, Pryor lost his title in 1985 due to inactivity. He lost the only fight of his career two years later in 1987 to Bobby Joe Young. He recorded three more wins in meaningless fights before retiring for good with a rec-ord of 39–1.

5.   KHAOSAI GALAXY

Known as the "Thai Tyson," Khaosai Galaxy domi-nated the junior bantamweight division from 1984 until his retirement in 1991. During that span, he defended the title nineteen times with sixteen kayoes. His only loss was in his seventh pro fight, against Sakda Sak-suree for the Thai bantamweight crown. He dropped a ten-round decision. Galaxy avenged the defeat a mere two months later by stopping Saksuree in the sixth round. He ended his career with a record of 50–1 with forty-four kayoes.

6.   PACKEY MCFARLAND

Packey McFarland, known as the "Pride of the Stock-yards" and the "Chicago Flash," fought from 1904 to 1915 as a lightweight, piling up win after win. His only loss came in his first year as a pro to Dusty Miller. He never got a second chance at Miller. After that McFar-land either won or fought in no-decision bouts. He fin-ished his career with a record of 64–1–5 with thirty-four no-decisions.

7. JAMES J. JEFFRIES

James J. Jeffries, largely overlooked today, was a fine heavyweight champion who reigned from 1899 to 1904 without defeat. He turned pro in 1896 and retired eight years later as the undefeated heavyweight champion. He twice defeated greats Bob Fitzsimmons and "Gentleman" James Corbett. When Jack Johnson became heavyweight champion, the public clamored for Jeffries to come out of retirement as "The Great White Hope" to wrest the title away from Johnson. Jeffries succumbed to the pressure and made an ill-fated comeback in 1910, losing badly to Johnson. He never fought again. His record was 18–1–2.

8. MYUNG-WOO YUH

Korea's Myung-Woo Yuh dominated the light flyweight division for nearly ten years. He captured the WBA belt in 1985 with a fifteen-round decision over Joey Olivo. He then made an astounding seventeen straight title defenses until he lost a twelve-round decision to Japan's Hiroki Ioka in 1991. He defeated Ioka in a rematch. He fought only one more fight, retiring with a record of 38–1.

9. YOKO GUSHIKEN

Japan's Yoko Gushiken, known as "Fierce Eagle," was a southpaw slugger who dominated the light flyweight division for the last half of the 1970s. He captured the WBA crown in 1976 and made fourteen successful defenses, nine by kayo. He retired in 1981 after losing the only bout of his career to Pedro Flores. His record was 23–1.

10. **TYRONE EVERETT**

Tyrone Everett—"Ty the Fly"—was a master boxer from Philadelphia who won thirty-four straight bouts heading into a world title shot for the WBC super featherweight title against champion Alfredo Escalera. Everett outboxed Escalera, winning at least ten of the rounds in the eyes of nearly all ringside observers. However, two judges somehow scored the bout for Escalera, ranking it as one of the worst decisions in boxing history. Everett never received another title shot as he was murdered while a rematch for the world title was pending. His record was 36–1.

Great Trilogies

Boxing history is filled with many great rivalries. Some of these rivalries treated boxing fans to three entertaining bouts. The following trilogies are considered among the best in the sport. In each of them, the fighters went into their third match with a victory apiece.

1. ALI–FRAZIER

Muhammad Ali's greatest rival in the boxing ring was "Smokin" Joe Frazier. The two first met in Madison Square Garden in March 1971, when Frazier was the undefeated champion and Ali the undefeated ex-champion returning from more than three years in exile. Frazier won a unanimous decision after dropping Ali in the final round. Ali won the second fight by a twelve-round unanimous decision in January 1974. Then, in October 1975, the two met in the classic war called the "Thrilla in Manila." Ali won the fight via a fourteenth-round technical knockout when Frazier's trainer, Eddie Futch, refused to let his valiant fighter take any further punishment. Ali later said that the fight in Manila was the closest thing to death that he had ever felt.

2. ZALE-GRAZIANO

From 1946 to 1948, Tony Zale and Rocky Graziano fought three brutal battles for the world middleweight title. Each fight was an all-out war with both men inflicting and suffering serious damage. In the first bout—a fight *The New York Times* called "one of the great fights of fistic history"—Zale dropped Graziano in the first round and Graziano returned the favor in the second. Graziano battered Zale nearly senseless in round five, but somehow Zale survived to stop Graziano in the sixth round. Graziano won the second bout in the sixth round. In the third fight, Zale kayoed Graziano in the third round to win back the belt.

3. ALI-NORTON

Perhaps the fighter who caused Muhammad Ali the most problems from a style standpoint was the awkward and strong Ken Norton. Norton burst onto the heavyweight scene with a twelve-round split-decision victory over Ali in March 1973. Ali suffered a broken jaw in the bout. Ali managed to eke out a split decision in a rematch later that year. The two met for the final time in Yankee Stadium in September 1976. Ali won the final round on all three scorecards to win a controversial but unanimous decision.

4. DURAN-DEJESUS

Before his storied rivalry at welterweight with Sugar Ray Leonard, Panama's Roberto "Hands of Stone" Duran faced off against the talented Puerto Rican Esteban DeJesus three times in the 1970s. In November 1972, DeJesus handed the 31–0 Duran his first defeat via a ten-round unanimous decision. DeJesus dropped

Duran in the opening round with his patented left hook. Duran avenged his sole defeat in March 1974 with an eleventh-round technical knockout, though DeJesus again dropped him in the first round. The rubber match occurred in January 1978 as a unification match. Duran held the WBA lightweight belt, while DeJesus held the WBC belt. Duran won via technical knockout in the twelfth round.

5. PATTERSON–JOHANSSON

Floyd Patterson and Ingemar Johansson squared off three times for the world heavyweight title from 1959 to 1961. Sweden's Johansson shocked the boxing establishment in the first fight, flooring Patterson seven times to win via technical knockout in the third round. Patterson won the second bout in the fifth round. The rubber match opened as a wild affair with both fighters hitting the canvas in the first round. Patterson prevailed in the sixth round.

6. GRIFFITH–PARET

Emile Griffith and Benny "Kid" Paret fought three times for the world welterweight title from 1961 to 1962. Griffith won the first match with a come-from-behind kayo in the thirteenth round. Paret regained the title with a controversial fifteen-round decision in the second bout. In the third fateful match, Griffith pounded a helpless Paret until referee Ruby Goldstein belatedly stopped the bout as Paret lay unconscious on the ropes. It was too late—Paret suffered a fatal head injury from the beating.

7. BOWE–HOLYFIELD

Riddick "Big Daddy" Bowe and Evander "The Real Deal" Holyfield gave boxing fans three memorable

wars in the 1990s. In November 1992, the two undefeated heavyweights clashed for Holyfield's title. Bowe
won a twelve-round unanimous decision and nearly
kayoed Holyfield in the tenth round. It was considered
the fight of the year. In November 1993, Holyfield regained his title by a twelve-round majority decision.
The fight is largely remembered for the bizarre actions
of the so-called Fan Man, a paraglider who parachuted
into the ring in the seventh round. In November 1995,
Bowe defeated Holyfield by a technical knockout in
their third bout in the eighth round. Holyfield dropped
Bowe in the sixth round before succumbing to his larger
foe.

8. ORTIZ–LAGUNA

Before Duran and DeJesus squared off in a Panama–
versus–Puerto Rico rivalry, Ismael Laguna and Carlos
Ortiz fought three fights that all went the full fifteen-
round distance for the world lightweight title. In April
1965, Laguna outboxed Ortiz to win a majority decision. Seven months later the aggressive Ortiz won a
fifteen-round decision, nearly stopping Laguna in the
late rounds. The two future Hall of Famers fought their
rubber match in April 1967. Ortiz won a fifteen-round
decision.

9. GONZALEZ–CARBAJAL

One of the most exciting trilogies occurred in the junior
flyweight division between Humberto "Chiquita" Gonzalez and Michael "Little Hands of Stone" Carbajal. In
the first bout, in 1993, Gonzalez dropped Carbajal twice
and was ahead on all three scorecards heading into the
seventh round. Then Carbajal landed a brutal left hook
that kayoed Gonzalez. It was everyone's fight of the

year. In 1994, the two rivals faced off twice, with Gonzalez winning two close decisions.

10. BENVENUTI-GRIFFITH

Italy's popular Nino Benvenuti earned his place in boxing history with his trilogy against the great Emile Griffith. Griffith, who already had achieved greatness at welterweight, held the middleweight crown when the two faced off for the first time in April 1967. Griffith dropped Benvenuti in the fourth round, but the Italian came back to win a fifteen-round decision. Griffith regained the title by fifteen-round decision by employing an effective body attack. In March 1968, Benvenuti won the rubber match via a fifteen-round decision.

Great Upsets in Heavyweight Title Bouts

Expert boxing commentator Larry Merchant has called boxing the "theatre of the unexpected." The description applies most dramatically when an underdog wins the most valued prize in the sport—the world heavyweight title. Most of the time it does not happen. The favored fighter wins. But sometimes the unthinkable happens. Just ask Buster Douglas. The following is a list of ten great upsets in the annals of heavyweight boxing history.

1. BUSTER DOUGLAS–MIKE TYSON (February 11, 1990)

Heavyweight champion "Iron" Mike Tyson had obliterated the heavyweight division in unifying the title before his twenty-second birthday. He was the epitome of dominance. But in February 1990 in Tokyo, Japan, he fell victim to perhaps the greatest upset in boxing history. Challenger James "Buster" Douglas, a career underachiever, fought the fight of his life, inspired by the recent death of his mother. Douglas controlled the action with his jab and straight right cross and survived a knockdown in the eighth round. The forty-two-to-one underdog stopped Tyson with a fusillade of heavy blows in the tenth round.

2. EVANDER HOLYFIELD–MIKE TYSON (November 9, 1996)

In 1996, Mike Tyson had regained the world heavyweight title after serving more than three years in an Indiana prison for rape. Experts expected him to dominate as he had in his first reign. In November 1996, his opponent was former champion Evander "The Real Deal" Holyfield. Holyfield was a great warrior, but the consensus was that he was past his prime and would be devoured by Tyson. Oddsmakers pegged him as a twenty-five-to-one underdog. They were wrong, as Holyfield outboxed Tyson and roughed him up on the inside. Tyson's strength waned considerably as the fight progressed, and he was stopped in the eleventh round.

3. CASSIUS CLAY–Sonny LISTON (February 25, 1964)

From the late 1950s until 1964, Charles "Sonny" Liston was perhaps the most feared heavyweight in history. He pummeled champion Floyd Patterson in successive one-round knockouts and was the undisputed king of the ring until he faced a loquacious braggart by the name of Cassius Marcellus Clay. Clay, the 1960 Olympic gold medalist at light heavyweight, possessed amazing speed and quickness. But few experts believed he could stand up to the mighty Liston. Clay was an eight-to-one underdog. In the fight in Miami Beach, Florida, Clay used his great hand and foot speed to frustrate Liston. Liston ended up quitting on his stool after the seventh round. Cassius Clay had indeed "shook up the world."

4. MUHAMMAD ALI–GEORGE FOREMAN
(October 30, 1974)

In 1974, George Foreman was not the happy George Foreman huckster of grills that he is today. He was viewed as a sullen monster of destruction, the second coming of Sonny Liston. His awe-inspiring power had obliterated Joe Frazier and Ken Norton. Thirty-something Muhammad Ali was to be his next victim in Kinshasa, Zaire. Ali employed his now famous "rope-a-dope" tactic to the dismay of his own corner. He leaned against the ropes and allowed Foreman to punch himself out. Amazingly, the strategy worked, and Ali stopped an exhausted Foreman in the eighth round.

5. JAMES J. BRADDOCK–MAX BAER (June 13, 1935)

James J. Braddock became one of the most unlikely heavyweight champions when in 1935 he outpointed the heavily favored Max Baer over fifteen rounds. Baer, who possessed a devastating right hand, had captured the title by pummeling Italian giant Primo Carnera. Braddock, who had a journeyman-like record, was viewed as a safe defense for Baer. He had lost a decision when he had fought for the world light heavyweight crown in 1929. Max, however, was a notorious playboy, and he did not train properly for the fight. Braddock easily outworked Baer to win a unanimous decision. Famous journalist Damon Runyon dubbed Braddock "The Cinderella Man" for his unlikely ascension to the heavyweight throne.

6. INGEMAR JOHANSSON–FLOYD PATTERSON
(June 26, 1959)

Sweden's Ingemar Johansson shocked the boxing establishment when he kayoed Floyd Patterson in June

1959 in New York to capture the heavyweight title. Patterson was in the prime of his career after successfully defending his title four times. His fifth defense against the unbeaten but relatively unknown Johansson was supposed to be routine. For two rounds, Patterson used his superior boxing skills, but in the third round Johansson landed an overhand right that floored the champion. Patterson gamely rose to his feet only to be knocked back down again. Finally, the referee stopped the fight after the seventh knockdown. Unfortunately for the Swede, his title reign was short-lived, as Patterson regained the title in a rematch. In the rubber match, Johansson floored Patterson twice in the first round, but Patterson rallied to stop Ingemar in the sixth round.

7. GENE TUNNEY–JACK DEMPSEY
(September 23, 1926)

In 1926, Jack Dempsey was a most popular heavyweight champion. The slugger nicknamed the "Manassa Mauler" was in a league with baseball's Babe Ruth as a hero of the masses. He won the title in 1919 and had defended it successfully five times. His next opponent was a former light heavyweight named Gene Tunney. Though Dempsey was a heavy favorite, Tunney believed he could outbox Dempsey. And that's exactly what he did. He stunned Dempsey in the first round on his way to an easy unanimous decision. Tunney also defeated Dempsey in their rematch in the famous "Long Count" bout. The bout was called such because in the seventh round, Dempsey dropped Tunney but failed to go into the nearest neutral corner. Tunney rose at the official count of nine even though he had actually been down about fourteen seconds. He proceeded to outbox Dempsey again.

8.   GEORGE FOREMAN–MICHAEL MOORER
(November 5, 1994)

Big George Foreman was a devastating force in the 1970s with kayo victories over Joe Frazier, Ken Norton, and Ron Lyle. However, after a points loss to defensive specialist Jimmy Young, Foreman retired from boxing and became a preacher. Then, in 1987, Foreman announced his comeback to the jeers of many boxing experts. For a few years, Foreman feasted on marginal opposition. However, people began to take notice when he pounded out Gerry Cooney in two rounds. Then, in 1992, he acquitted himself well in losing a unanimous decision to Evander Holyfield. But in 1994, Foreman lost to Tommy Morrison and seemed an unlikely candidate to unseat Michael Moorer, the undefeated champion who had defeated Holyfield to become the first southpaw heavyweight champion. Moorer's handlers believed Foreman would be a relatively safe choice for a first defense. They were correct for nine and a half rounds. Moorer's trainer, Teddy Atlas, even told his fighter that his sparring partners were better than the plodding Foreman after the first round. But Atlas also warned Moorer not to stand right in front of Foreman and trade punches. In the tenth round, Foreman landed a chopping right hand, and the forty-five-year-old regained the heavyweight title that he had lost twenty-two years earlier in Zaire to Muhammad Ali.

9.   MICHAEL SPINKS–LARRY HOLMES
(September 21, 1985)

In 1985, heavyweight champion Larry Holmes stood at 48–0 and had lorded over the division since 1978 with perhaps the finest left jab in all of boxing. Though signs of age had begun to appear, Holmes was favored to tie Rocky Marciano's venerable 49–0 mark in his next defense against Michael Spinks, the undefeated former light heavyweight champion. Spinks sought to accomplish what many great light heavyweights before him, champions such as Billy Conn and Bob Foster, could not do—beat the heavyweight champion. To the amazement of many, the unorthodox Spinks managed to frustrate Holmes and captured a close but unanimous decision. Spinks also won a rematch, though many believed Holmes was robbed.

10. HASIM RAHMAN–LENNOX LEWIS (April 22, 2001)

In early 2001, Lennox Lewis had established himself as the premier heavyweight in the world. Many experts began considering him one of the truly great heavyweight champions. He had twice defeated Evander Holyfield (though his first victory was officially declared a draw in one of the worst decisions in history) and had also beaten the dangerous David Tua. It appeared his reign would be safe when the champion signed to face Hasim Rahman, a decent enough fighter who had suffered knockout losses to Tua and Oleg Maskaev. Apparently, Lewis believed too much of his own press and even spent time on a movie set a week before the fight in Johannesburg, South Africa. Lewis appeared to be slowly seizing control of the action, but in the fifth round Rahman landed a right hand and Lewis fell like a sack of potatoes and could not beat the count. To his credit, Lewis kayoed Rahman in a rematch in November 2001 with an equally devastating punch.

Come-from-Behind Kayoes

Basketball coach Dick Motta once said, "The opera ain't over till the fat lady sings." Well, the same principle applies in boxing because the fight isn't over until the final bell rings. Part of boxing's great intrigue is that a fighter hopelessly behind on points can still pull out the victory with a single kayo punch. In football or basketball, when a team is twenty points behind with a few minutes left, the game is over. People leave the stands. But in boxing a fighter can lose every single round and then triumph with a single punch. In the following bouts, a fighter behind on points came up with a needed knockout to win the bout.

1. JAKE LAMOTTA–LAURENT DAUTHUILLE (September 13, 1950)

Styles make fights, and some fighters simply have the right style to beat what most would consider to be a better fighter. Such was the case with slick Frenchman boxer Laurent Dauthuille and rugged American brawler Jake LaMotta. LaMotta was the much better fighter, having handed the great Sugar Ray Robinson his first defeat. But Dauthuille matched up well with LaMotta and defeated him in a ten-round decision in February 1949. When LaMotta won the world middleweight title a year later, he signed to fight the Frenchman to avenge his earlier defeat. The rematch occurred at Olympia Stadium in Detroit and followed a similar pattern to the first bout. For more than fourteen rounds, Dauthuille outboxed LaMotta for a commanding lead on all three judges' scorecards. But in the final round, LaMotta scored a miraculous kayo to stop the Frenchman with only thirteen seconds remaining in the fight.

2. **MIKE WEAVER–JOHN TATE (March 3, 1980)**

In 1980, "Big" John Tate looked like the promising heavyweight of the future. He was big, strong, and undefeated, with decent boxing skills. He had just captured the vacant WBA world heavyweight title with a convincing points win over South Africa's Gerrie Coetzee in South Africa. His first defense looked routine. He was slated to fight Mike Weaver, a fighter with a record of 21–9. Weaver's only claim to fame had been giving WBC champ Larry Holmes a tough fight the year before. Tate dominated much of the fight with his boxing skills. Heading into the final round, he was comfortably ahead on all three judges' scorecards. By most accounts, he had won at least ten of the previous rounds. All he had to do was finish the fight on his feet. Then, with only forty-five seconds to go until the final bell, Weaver threw a big left hook. It landed flush on Tate's jaw and produced a *Rocky*-like kayo. Tate fell in slow motion to the canvas and never even quivered as the ten-count was tolled. Mike "Hercules" Weaver became a most unlikely heavyweight champion.

3. GEORGE FOREMAN–MICHAEL MOORER (November 5, 1994)

In November 1994, Michael Moorer stood at 36–0 and was coming off a surprise victory over Evander Holyfield for the WBA and IBF world title belts. The former light heavyweight champ had become the first southpaw to win the heavyweight crown. In his first defense, he signed to fight forty-five-year-old "Big" George Foreman, who had just lost a unanimous decision to Tommy "The Duke" Morrison. For nine and a half rounds, it was a relatively easy fight for the champion. He controlled the action with his quicker hands and effective right jab. Foremen seemed too old to let his punches go. Heading into the tenth round, Moorer was pitching a virtual shutout. It appeared that Foreman should have stuck with broadcasting with his fellow HBO fight commentators Larry Merchant and Jim Lampley, who said so during the bout. Then, in the tenth round, the ever-plodding Foreman landed a short chopping right hand that stunned the champion. Foreman followed with another right hand on Moorer's chin that felled the champion. Moorer did not beat the count, and George Foreman became the oldest and perhaps most improbable heavyweight champion, capturing the title twenty-two years after his first title. As Lampley would exclaim, "My God, he's done it!"

4. JOE LOUIS–BILLY CONN I (June 18, 1941)

In 1941, Joe Louis had already earned a place in ring history as a great heavyweight champion. His record stood at 56–1, and he was widely believed to be invincible. In June 1941, he entered the ring against an opponent he outweighed by thirty pounds. Pittsburgh's popular Billy Conn had abandoned his world light heavyweight title to pursue the sport's ultimate prize. In New York's Polo Grounds, Conn fought the fight of his life for twelve rounds, as his speed and elusiveness clearly bothered Louis. Heading into the thirteenth round, Conn was ahead on two cards and even on the third. Believing he had hurt Louis in the previous round, Conn went for the knockout. Conn's reckless aggressiveness gave "The Brown Bomber" the opportunity he needed, and the champion landed a devastating right hand to Conn's jaw. The fight was over. Years later, Conn would still rue his mistake. In Peter Heller's *In This Corner . . . !*, Conn said: "You only get one chance. Of all the times to be a wise guy, I had to pick it against him to be a wise guy. Serves me right."

5. JERSEY JOE WALCOTT–ROCKY MARCIANO (September 23, 1952)

In September 1952, heavyweight champion Jersey Joe Walcott defended his crown against the undefeated Rocky Marciano in Philadelphia's Municipal Stadium. Walcott, a clever boxer with fancy footwork, stunned Marciano with a left hook that deposited the "Brockton Blockbuster" on the canvas. Marciano rose at the count of five and continued to press forward. The two men traded punishment for much of the fight. Heading into the thirteenth round, Walcott was ahead on all three scorecards. Then Marciano landed his vaunted "Susie-Q," his short, compact right-hand punch that produced many of his kayoes. The shot of that right hand contorting Walcott's jaw endures as one of the great ring photos of all time. The punch also spelled the end of Walcott's reign as champion.

6. **MELDRICK TAYLOR–JULIO CESAR CHAVEZ** (March 17, 1990)

This clash of unbeaten champions in the junior welter-weight division may forever be remembered more for its controversial ending than for the thrilling drama it provided for nearly twelve rounds. American Meldrick Taylor, a former gold medalist, was 24–0–1 and the IBF champ. Julio Cesar Chavez, Mexico's number-one fighter, entered the ring in Las Vegas as the WBC champion with a record of 68–0. Taylor's blazing hand speed enabled him to build a points lead on the re-sourceful Chavez. Even though Chavez inflicted dam-aging body blows, Taylor's combination punching had him ahead on two of the three judges' scorecards head-ing into the twelfth and final round. Chavez needed a miracle—and he got it. With literally seconds to go, he pinned Taylor in the corner and pounded him to the ground. Taylor rose to his feet, but, with only two sec-onds remaining in the bout, referee Richard Steele stopped the fight. If Steele had allowed Taylor to finish out the two seconds, he would have won a split deci-sion. Instead, Chavez continued his unbeaten streak that was to last until 1994. Taylor went on to win a ver-sion of the welterweight title, but he was never the same fighter.

7. **THOMAS HEARNS–SUGAR RAY LEONARD** (September 16, 1981)

Many fight fans remember the early 1980s as a golden age for the welterweight division. Two of the major rea-sons for that are Sugar Ray Leonard and Thomas "Hit-man" Hearns. In September 1981, the two champions squared off in Las Vegas, Nevada, to unify the title.

Leonard, at 30–1, held the WBC belt, while Hearns, at 32–0, held the WBA title. Many pundits saw the bout as Leonard the boxer versus Hearns the puncher. In fact, Hearns showed his boxing skills, using his superior height and reach to frustrate Leonard for much of the bout. Heading into the fourteenth round, Leonard was behind on all three scorecards. His legendary trainer, Angelo Dundee, told him in the corner: "You're blowing it, kid!" But Leonard showed his greatness, pinning Hearns against the ropes to hand the "Hitman" his first defeat. The two would face off again in 1989, with Hearns dropping Leonard twice in the bout but getting only a disputed draw.

8. LEE ROY MURPHY–CHISANDA MUTTI (October 19, 1985)

In October 1985, Lee Roy "Solid Gold" Murphy defended his IBF cruiserweight title against unheralded challenger Chisanda Mutti at Louis II Stadium in Monte Carlo. Murphy, a former amateur great denied his chance at a gold medal because of the 1980 boycott of the Moscow Olympics, was making his second defense of his crown. Mutti took the fight to Murphy for much of the bout and was ahead on the cards going into the twelfth and final round. Then, a *Rocky II* moment happened that would have pleased the fans of Rocky Balboa and Apollo Creed. Both fighters landed powerful blows simultaneously and went down. Murphy rose to his feet on time and Mutti did not.

9. DAVID REID–ALFREDO DUVERGAL (August 4, 1996)

The 1996 Olympic Games were not looking good for the American boxing squad, as it faced the country's first gold-medal shutout since 1948. The light middle-weight final did not look very promising, either. Philadelphia's David Reid was losing to the heavily favored Cuban Alfredo Duvergal. In the third and final round, Reid was trailing 15–5 on the scorecards. Then Reid landed what has been called the most dramatic punch in U.S. Olympic boxing history. With a single punch, David Reid won the U.S.A.'s only gold medal of the Atlanta Games.

10. DAVID TUA

Heavyweight contender David Tua, the Samoan New Zealander, deserves special recognition in this category for multiple come-from-behind kayoes in his career. Though standing only 5'10", Tua, who sometimes

Chris Cozzone

David Tua has made a habit of come-from-behind kayoes, finishing off many opponents with his devastating left hook while behind on the scorecard.

weighs more than 250 pounds, possesses frightening power in his left hook. Many times in his career he has snatched victory from the jaws of defeat with crushing kayoes. He stopped David Izon in the twelfth round and Oleg Maskaev in the eleventh round with his patented left hook. In each of the fights, the decision was still in doubt. In December 1998, he was losing badly on the scorecards to Hasim Rahman when he landed a big left hook at the end of the round. Rahman, ahead by as many as seven points on one of the scorecards, could not recover, and Tua finished him in the tenth round. In 2002, Tua kayoed Fres Oquendo in the ninth round with a single left hook after trailing on all three scorecards. Suffice it to say that David Tua and his big left hook are never out of a fight until the final bell sounds.

Most Title Defenses

Very few boxers ever win world titles even in this age of alphabet soup in which there are multiple sanctioning bodies offering world title belts. Even fewer champions manage to keep their title for an extended period of time. The fighters on this list are the exception, as they each made numerous title defenses.

1. JOE LOUIS

The great "Brown Bomber" set a record for successful title defenses that has never been broken. He defended his world heavyweight crown an astounding twenty-five times from 1937 until 1949. His title defenses became so routine that some of his opponents were referred to collectively as members of the champion's "Bum of the Month" club.

2. RICARDO LOPEZ

Mexico's Ricardo "Finito" Lopez dominated the strawweight division, holding the WBC title from 1990 to 1999 and making an astonishing twenty-one successful defenses. He also won a junior flyweight world title. He never lost in his pro career, finishing with a record of 51–0–1 with thirty-eight knockouts. He announced his retirement in late 2002.

3. LARRY HOLMES

Larry Holmes, the "Easton Assassin," dominated the heavyweight division from 1978 to 1985, making twenty successful title defenses before finally losing a controversial decision to Michael Spinks. Seventeen of those defenses were of his WBC belt, which he first captured with a thrilling win over Ken Norton. Holmes was stripped of his WBC crown for failing to face the WBC's mandatory contender. The newly formed International Boxing Federation (IBF) named Holmes its champion, and he defended that title three times before losing to Spinks.

4. HENRY ARMSTRONG

The great Henry Armstrong was the only fighter in boxing history to hold world titles in three different divisions at the same time. In 1938, he held the featherweight, lightweight, and welterweight titles simultaneously. He made nineteen defenses of his welterweight crown, which he won in 1938 from Barney Ross. Armstrong defended his title frequently, making eleven defenses in 1939 alone. He finally lost in October 1940 on points to Fritzie Zivic.

5. KHAOSAI GALAXY

Thailand's Khaosai Galaxy made nineteen successful defenses of the WBA junior bantamweight crown he captured in November 1984. Sixteen of them came by knockout for the dominant little warrior called the "Thai Tyson." His last defense came in December 1991, and he retired with a record of 50–1 with forty-four kayoes.

6. RATANAPOL VORAPIN

Thailand's Ratanapol Sol Vorapin made nineteen successful defenses of the IBF strawweight crown that he won in 1992. He finally lost to South African Zolani Petelo in December 1997. Vorapin's great career has been overshadowed by the sheer dominance of Ricardo Lopez, who defeated Vorapin via a third-round technical knockout in December 2000. Vorapin never fought again, retiring with a record of 38–6–1.

7. EUSEBIO PEDROZA

Panama's Eusebio Pedroza made nineteen successful defenses of his WBA featherweight belt from 1978 to 1985 before finally surrendering the belt on points to Barry McGuigan over fifteen rounds. During his reign, Pedroza defeated many solid contenders, including Juan LaPorte and Rocky Lockridge (twice). He was elected to the International Boxing Hall of Fame in 1999.

8. MYUNG-WOO YUH

Korea's Myung-Woo Yuh made seventeen successful defenses of his WBA junior flyweight title. He won the title in December 1985 with a fifteen-round decision over Joey Olivo and did not relinquish it until a 1991 points loss to Japan's Hiroki Ioka. Yuh promptly regained the title from Ioka the next year. After making one more successful defense, he retired with a record of 38–1.

9. WILFREDO GOMEZ

Puerto Rico's power-punching Wilfredo Gomez made seventeen successful defenses of the WBC super bantamweight title he won in May 1977 over Dong-Kyun

Yum. He made his final defense with a fourteenth-round stoppage over tough Lupe Pintor in a classic battle. After that win, Gomez relinquished his title to campaign as a featherweight. He won the WBC featherweight title with a decision win over Juan LaPorte but lost the belt in his first defense against future great Azumah Nelson.

10. **SVEN OTTKE**

By October 2003, German Sven Ottke had made nineteen successful defenses of the IBF super middleweight title that he captured with a close twelve-round decision over Charles Brewer in October 1998. He added the WBA belt in March 2003. Ottke is a clever boxer who usually wins by decision, and he sports an unblemished mark of 32–0.

Greatest Punchers

Everybody loves to see a knockout. It is boxing's answer to a grand slam in baseball. The following fighters scored many knockouts when they laid leather on their opponents.

1. EARNIE SHAVERS

Earnie Shavers is, in the opinion of many, the hardest puncher of all time. Voted "Puncher of the Century" by the International Boxing Association, Shavers packed dynamite in his right hand. Earnie shaved his head and grew a Fu Manchu mustache that gave him the look of a Mongolian warrior. Shavers scored first-round kayoes over former heavyweight champions Ken Norton and Jimmy Ellis. He had a stretch of twenty-seven consecutive knockout victories during his run at the heavyweight throne. Shavers used to intimidate opponents at the weigh-in by shedding his shirt and fixing them with a cold, menacing stare. Shavers was so intimidating that he had a few opponents weigh in on the day of the bout and then not show up for the fight. One opponent was so frightened that he pleaded with the promoter for life insurance coverage minutes before entering the ring against Shavers. Former heavyweight champion Larry Holmes said Shavers hit him harder than any other ring opponent.

2. JACK DEMPSEY

Known as the "Manassa Mauler," Jack Dempsey kay-oed fifty of the sixty opponents he defeated. Dempsey packed dynamite in both hands, but his left hook was his most lethal punch. He would work his way inside an opponent's guard and fire away, attempting to land his left hook and close the show. During Dempsey's best years, from 1918 to 1923, he went 32–0 with twenty-eight knockouts—seventeen coming in the first round. The all-time great knocked out several world-class fighters including Jess Willard, Luis Angel Firpo, Bill Brennan, Jack Sharkey, Battling Levinsky, and "Gun-boat" Smith.

3. SUGAR RAY ROBINSON

Though also known as a skilled boxer, Sugar Ray Robinson registered 109 knockouts in his legendary career against many of the game's top boxers including Rocky Graziano, Jake LaMotta, Gene Fullmer, Bobo Olson, and Fritzie Zivic. Robinson threw rapid-fire combinations and took his punch with him when he moved up in weight from welterweight to middleweight. He became the first man to legitimately stop the granite-jawed Jake LaMotta, who later admitted throwing an earlier bout to Billy Fox. Five months after losing his middleweight title against Gene Fullmer in 1957, Sugar Ray regained his belt by knocking out Fullmer with a left hook in the fifth round of the rematch. Many consider that left hook to be the perfect punch.

4. SANDY SADDLER

Sandy Saddler scored 103 knockouts among his 144 victories. Unusually tall for a featherweight at 5'8", Saddler used his superior jab to set up his powerful left uppercuts and hooks that led to many knockouts. Saddler also had a tremendous right cross. Saddler is remembered for his four-bout, foul-infested series of matches with Willie Pep, of which Saddler won three.

5. HENRY ARMSTRONG

Henry Armstrong was known as "Hurricane Henry" or "Homicide Hank" for his nonstop punching offensive attack. The only boxer ever to hold titles in three weight divisions simultaneously, he was a lethal puncher who scored ninety-seven knockouts in his brilliant career. Armstrong had an abnormal heartbeat, which may have let him fight at such a breathtaking pace without concern for fatigue.

6. ARCHIE MOORE

No one knows for sure just how many stoppage victories boxing's all-time knockout leader has registered. As Archie himself said, "They lost a few along the way," referring to his days in the Civilian Conservation Corps when Archie competed in professional bouts in Arkansas in 1935, before resuming his amateur career after relocating to Missouri. Moore was a solid puncher with either hand and knocked out such world-class fighters as Yvon Durelle, Bobo Olson, Jimmy Bivins, Lloyd Marshall, and Holman Williams. In a challenge for the heavyweight title on September 21, 1955, Moore decked Rocky Marciano in the second round with a right hand before eventually succumbing to Marciano's power shots. Officially, Moore is credited with 131 knockouts.

7. ROCKY MARCIANO

Forty-three of Rocky Marciano's forty-nine victories in his unbeaten career came inside the distance, many of them via his famed right-hand knockout punch called the "Susie-Q." The Rock had tremendous stamina and recuperative powers. Rocky was down early in title defenses against Jersey Joe Walcott and Archie Moore but rallied to kayo both opponents. Marciano had short but powerful legs that launched his famed knockout power.

8. JOE LOUIS

Joe Louis had power in both hands. He was so devastating that his stiff left jab was as hard as most other heavyweights' power shots. He kayoed many opponents with a single punch, often his lethal right cross. The "Brown Bomber" scored fifty-four knockouts in his sixty-nine victories, with his list of victims reading as a "Who's Who" of former greats, including Max Schmeling, Max Baer, Jersey Joe Walcott, Primo Carnera, and Billy Conn. In his record twenty-five title defenses, only three challengers managed to even last the distance with Louis. "When you're hit by Louis, it's like a lightbulb breaking in your face," said James J. Braddock after his kayo loss to Louis.

9. MAX BAER

Nicknamed the "Clown Prince of Boxing" for his antics in and out of the ring, Baer was known to blow kisses to women at ringside in the middle of a fight. Baer had a vicious right hand that brought him knockouts over

Max Schmeling and Primo Carnera. Baer stopped Carnera to win the title in the eleventh round, putting Primo down eleven times before the contest was halted.

10.   JULIAN JACKSON

Julian Jackson was a junior middleweight and middle-weight champion of the late 1980s and early 1990s who possessed frightening one-punch power. He kay-oed Terry Norris and Herol Graham with single shots. He retired in 1998 with a record of 55–6 with forty-nine knockouts.

Youngest Champions

There are prodigies in every sport, and boxing is no exception. Most fighters spend several years in the amateur ranks honing and seasoning their skills fighting in three-round bouts. Today, many jurisdictions have strict age limits that prohibit a fighter from turning pro until he is eighteen. But in boxing history some fighters turned pro when they were barely teenagers. A precocious few were able to win world titles when they were very young. The following ten fighters deserve to be called prodigies because they accomplished so much at a young age.

1. WILFRED BENITEZ

Wilfred Benitez shocked the boxing world when he defeated the legendary Antonio "Kid Pambele" Cervantes over fifteen rounds to win the WBA world junior welterweight title on March 6, 1976, becoming the youngest world champion ever at age seventeen. Benitez turned pro at age thirteen and won titles in three different weight classes by the time he was twenty-two. He won the welterweight title with a decision over Carlos Palomino and the junior middleweight title with a one-punch kayo over Maurice Hope. He also defeated the one and only Roberto Duran.

2. TERRY MCGOVERN

"Terrible" Terry McGovern turned pro at age seventeen in 1897 and took only two years to win the world bantamweight title at age nineteen with a victory over previously unbeaten Tom (Pedlar) Palmer. McGovern won the world featherweight title in 1900 with a win over George Dixon. He also defeated world lightweight titleholder Frank Erne in a nontitle bout.

3. PIPINO CUEVAS

Mexico's Pipino Cuevas turned pro in 1971 at the tender age of fourteen. Though he was stopped in his pro debut, Cuevas won the WBA world welterweight championship in July 1977 against Angel Espada when he was eighteen years old. He defended his title eleven times until he faced Thomas "The Hitman" Hearns.

4. TONY CANZONERI

Tony Canzoneri turned pro at age sixteen in New York. When he was nineteen, he outpointed Johnny Dundee over fifteen rounds in October 1927 to win the world featherweight championship. He later won world titles in the lightweight and junior welterweight divisions. He defeated such great fighters as Kid Chocolate, Jackie Berg, and Jimmy McLarnin.

5. NETRNOI VORASINGH

Netrnoi Vorasingh turned pro before his sixteenth birthday in 1975 in his homeland of Thailand. He captured the WBC light flyweight title in May 1978 when he was nineteen years of age. He lost the title in his second title defense. He later died in a motorcycle accident when he was twenty-three.

6. MIKE TYSON

Whatever else can be said about Mike Tyson, he remains the youngest man to ever win the world heavyweight title. In November 1986, he kayoed Trevor Berbick in the second round to win the WBC world heavyweight crown at the tender age of twenty. He later defeated James "Bonecrusher" Smith for the WBA crown and Tony "TNT" Tucker for the IBF crown, earning universal recognition before his twenty-second birthday.

7. BEN VILLAFLOR

The Philippines' Ben Villaflor turned pro at the tender age of fourteen. When he was nineteen, he defeated Alfredo Marcano in April 1972 to win the WBA super featherweight title. He regained the belt in October 1973 with a first-round kayo over Kuniaki Shibata. After defending his title five times, he retired in 1976 after dropping a fifteen-round decision to Samuel Serrano.

8. MANDO RAMOS

The talented Mando Ramos became the youngest world lightweight champion with an eleventh-round TKO victory over Carlos Cruz in February 1969. Ramos was only twenty years of age. He had lost a fifteen-round decision to Cruz in 1968. He would again win a world title in 1972 with a fifteen-round decision win over Pedro Carrasco.

9. **HIROKI IOKA**

Japan's Hiroki Ioka won the WBC minimumweight title in October 1987 in only his ninth pro bout when he was nineteen years of age. He would later move up to the light flyweight division and add a second world title in 1991. He failed in three attempts to add a world flyweight title and one attempt at the super flyweight title. He last fought in 1998.

10. **FLOYD PATTERSON**

Floyd Patterson became the youngest world heavyweight champion at the time he won the title in 1956 with a fifth-round stoppage of Archie Moore. He was only twenty-one years old. His record stood for thirty years until Mike Tyson won the crown in 1986 at twenty. Patterson was also the first man to win the world heavyweight crown twice. In 1959, he lost his crown to Sweden's Ingemar Johansson. He regained the title from Johansson in 1960.

No Time to Waste for World Title

M ost fighters with potential begin their pro careers
slowly. They face an assortment of lesser fighters
to build confidence and gain experience. But a few
fighters eschew this traditional path of development
and receive a world title shot much earlier in their careers.

A prime example was 1956 Olympic heavyweight
gold medalist Pete Rademacher. In his pro debut, Rademacher challenged world heavyweight champion
Floyd Patterson. This was virtually unheard of in boxing
circles, as boxers simply don't fight for world titles in
their pro debuts. Rademacher lost via sixth-round kayo
and never received another world title shot. Much earlier, Jack Skelly fought his first pro fight in 1892
against champion George Dixon for the world featherweight title. Dixon stopped Skelly in the eighth round.
The following are ten fighters who won a world title with
little professional experience under their belts. Most of
the fighters come from the lower weight classes, and
many are from the Far East.

1. SAENSAK MUANGSURIN

Unbelievably, Saensak Muangsurin of Thailand captured the World Boxing Council junior welterweight

championship in only his third professional bout. In 1975, he stopped Perico Fernandez in the tenth round to win the crown. He lost and regained the title with consecutive bouts in 1976 against Miguel Velasquez. After regaining the title, the power-punching Muang-surin made seven consecutive defenses of his title before losing to Sang-Hyun Kim in 1978. He retired with a record of 14–6.

2. LEOn SPInKS

Leon Spinks captured a gold medal in the light heavyweight division at the 1976 Olympic Games in Montreal. When he turned pro, Spinks's management team wasted little time in moving Spinks up the ladder. In only his eighth pro bout, he faced the great Muhammad Ali for the world heavyweight title. Spinks won a split-decision victory in a monumental upset. His reign was a short one as Ali defeated him in a rematch. Spinks's career was mostly downhill from there, and he eventually became a journeyman, finishing with a record of 26–17–3.

3. JEFF FEnECH

Australian Jeff Fenech won the International Boxing Federation's bantamweight crown in 1985 in only his seventh pro bout. He stopped Satoshi Shingaki in the ninth round. Fenech's nonstop attack led him to titles in three different divisions—bantamweight, junior featherweight, and featherweight. Only a terrible decision prevented him from adding a world super featherweight title to his resume. Most ringside observers felt he clearly deserved better than the draw he received against the great Azumah Nelson in 1991. He retired after a losing effort for a world lightweight title in 1996.

He was elected to the International Boxing Hall of Fame in 2002.

4. DAVEY MOORE

In 1982, Davey Moore won the World Boxing Association's junior middleweight championship in only his ninth pro bout. He stopped Tidashi Mihari in the sixth round to capture the belt. He successfully defended his crown three times before he faced the legendary Roberto "Hands of Stone" Duran in 1983. Duran punished Moore over eight rounds to win the title. Moore earned another shot at the world championship in 1986 but lost to Buster Drayton in the tenth round. Moore began a comeback in 1988, winning two fights. He planned to fight for another world title, but it was not to be. Moore died at the age of twenty-eight when he slipped and fell under his moving Jeep.

5. SOT CHITALADA

Thailand's Sot Chitalada fought for the World Boxing Council's junior flyweight championship in only his fifth pro bout. He lost a fifteen-round decision to Jung-Koo Chang in March 1984. Undeterred, Chitalada moved up to the flyweight division. In his eighth pro bout, he won a twelve-round decision over Gabriel Bernal in September 1984 to win the WBC flyweight title. He successfully defended his title six times before losing in 1988 to Yong Kang Kim. In 1989, Chitalada regained the title by winning a twelve-round split decision rematch over Kim. He defended the title four times during his second reign. He lost his title to Muangchai Kittikasem in 1991. He retired after losing again to Kittikasem in 1992.

6. **MUANGCHAI KITTIKASEM**

Muangchai Kittikasem, another great fighter from Thailand, won the International Boxing Federation's junior flyweight championship in only his seventh pro bout. He won a twelve-round split decision over Tacy Macalos. He made three successful defenses before facing American dynamo Michael Carbajal, who stopped Kittikasem in the seventh round. Kittikasem moved up a weight class to flyweight and defeated fellow countryman Sot Chitalada for a world title. He defended that title three times before falling to Russian star Yuri Arbachakov. Kittikasem retired in 1996. He came back in 1999 for a fight in Tokyo, Japan. He retired for good after losing.

7. **CHAN-HEE PARK**

Chan-Hee Park of Korea captured the World Boxing Council's world flyweight championship in 1979 by defeating legendary Hall of Famer Miguel Canto over fifteen rounds. It was only Park's eleventh pro fight. Park made five successful defenses of his crown before losing to Japan's Shoji Oguma. Park would lose two more decisions to Oguma in world title bouts. He retired with a record of 17–6.

8. **HILARIO ZAPATA**

Panama's legendary little southpaw Hilario Zapata dominated the lighter weight divisions in the 1980s. In March 1980, Zapata decisioned Shigeo Nakajima over fifteen rounds to win the WBC world junior flyweight championship. It was only his twelfth pro bout. Zapata made eight successful defenses of his crown before losing to Armado Ursua in 1982. He regained his title in

1982 and made two more successful defenses. In 1985, Zapata decisioned Alonzo Gonzalez to win the WBA flyweight crown. He defended his title five times before losing in 1987 to Fidel Bassa. Zapata finally retired in 1993 after a failed attempt for a world super flyweight title.

9. JUNG-IL BYUN

Korea's Jung-Il Byun won the WBC world bantamweight title in March 1993 with a unanimous decision victory over the more experienced Victor Rabanales. It was only Byun's ninth pro bout. He made one successful defense before being stripped of his crown in October 1993. He lost a twelve-round split decision to Japan's Yasuei Yakushiji in his opponent's home country for the vacant title. He retired after losing again to Yakushiji in a rematch.

10. HIROKI IOKA

Japan's Hiroki Ioka won the WBC minimumweight championship in October 1987 with a twelve-round decision over Mai Thomburifarm. It was only Ioka's ninth pro bout. He defended his title twice before losing to Napa Kiatwanchai. In 1991, Ioka captured the WBA light flyweight title with a twelve-round decision over the undefeated Myung-Woo Yuh. He defended his title twice before losing to Yuh in a rematch. Ioka doggedly pursued another world title, receiving four more title shots. He lost them all and retired in 1998.

Great Fighters Who Never Fought for a Belt

B oxing fans have been blessed to see or read about many great world champions. But some great pugilists never received a chance to win a title. Whether it was racism, politics, or simply because they were too good for their own good, many deserving fighters never got their chance at glory. Many of the boxers on this list were great African-American pugilists denied their opportunity by what the great writer W.E.B. DuBois called the "Veil" of race.

Simply stated, the color line prevented many great African-American fighters from fighting for a white champion's belt. This list includes four African-American boxers who never received a shot at the world heavyweight crown—Sam Langford, Harry Wills, Joe Jeanette, and Sam McVey. All have been elected to the International Boxing Hall of Fame.

Other boxers were denied title shots because champions or their managers figured out ways to avoid facing them in the ring. Politics has always played a large role in boxing. Some fighters simply are avoided because they are feared. Many light heavyweight champions avoided the great Archie Moore for many years because he was so good. More recently, Marvelous Marvin Hagler had to wait years before finally receiving his shot at the world middleweight championship.

1. SAM LANGFORD

Known as the "Boston Tar Baby," Sam Langford fought in every weight class from lightweight to heavyweight from 1902 to 1926. He fought the best of the black fighters and any white fighter who would fight him. But he never received a world title shot. Racism was the only reason Langford never won a world title. Blocked by the color bar, Langford fought fellow black greats of his day Harry Wills, Sam McVey, and Joe Jeanette numerous times. Even the great Jack Johnson refused to fight Langford when Johnson was world heavyweight champion.

2. PETER JACKSON

Australian Peter Jackson, a black man born in the Virgin Islands, was the best fighter of his generation. Only racism kept him from receiving a shot at the world heavyweight championship. John L. Sullivan, the first recognized modern world heavyweight champion, refused to fight a black fighter for racial reasons. Sullivan declared: "I will not fight a Negro. I never have, and I never shall."

"Gentleman" James Corbett, who defeated Sullivan for the world title, said that Jackson was the best heavyweight he had ever seen. Corbett earned his title shot at Sullivan by battling Jackson to a sixty-one-round draw. Jackson pleaded for a rematch with Corbett when Gentleman Jim was world champion, but Corbett declined. Jackson ended his career with a mark of thirty-five wins, only three losses, and one draw.

3. CHARLEY BURLEY

Charles Duane Burley dominated the welterweight and middleweight divisions during the late 1930s and 1940s but never received a title shot. World champions avoided him like the Black Plague—which is perhaps how many managers viewed this African-American great.

Some maintain that even the great Sugar Ray Robinson, who most boxing historians rank as the greatest boxer pound-for-pound in history, wanted no part of Charley Burley. Burley often battled much larger men, even heavyweights who outweighed him by more than fifty pounds. Legendary trainer Eddie Futch once said that Charley Burley was the best fighter he ever saw. The legendary Archie Moore, who had more than 230 pro bouts, ranked Burley as the toughest fighter he ever faced.

4. HARRY WILLS

Known as the "Black Panther," Harry Wills stalked the heavyweight division from 1910 to 1932. After Jack Johnson, the first African-American world heavyweight champion, had infuriated much of white America, people simply weren't ready to accept another African-American as champion. Thus, Wills was denied his opportunity.

Jack Dempsey, the charismatic brawler who was world champion in the early- to mid-1920s, refused to get in the ring with the 6'2", 220-pound Wills. Wills had to fight numerous bouts against other black heavyweights of his day, including Sam Langford.

5. **LASZLO PAPP**

Laszlo Papp won gold medals for his native Hungary in the 1948, 1952, and 1956 Olympic Games. In 1957, he turned professional and never lost a bout, compiling a record of 27–0–2 from 1957 to 1964. His two draws were to a French fighter in a Paris bout and an Italian fighter in a Milan bout.

Rumors of a world title bout circulated in 1965, but it was not to be. The Communist-controlled government of Hungary refused to let Papp fight just as he was on the verge of a world title shot against American Joey Giardiello. The official announcement read that his "professional career would not be compatible with our socialist principles." Papp disagreed with the government's decision but complied and served many years as coach of the Hungarian boxing team.

6. **KID NORFOLK**

In today's boxing world, Kid Norfolk would be a light heavyweight superstar. But in the 1910s and '20s, he was just another black fighter who could not hurdle the color bar. Born William Ward, his manager dubbed him Kid Norfolk because he hailed from Norfolk, Virginia. He defeated such Hall of Fame greats as Harry Greb, Battling Siki, and Billy Miske. Norfolk claimed to be world light heavyweight champion after defeating Miske in 1917, but the boxing world did not recognize him.

7. **JIMMY BIVINS**

Jimmy Bivins fought from 1940 to 1955 in the welterweight, middleweight, light heavyweight, and heavyweight divisions. He defeated many future and former

world champions. In 1942, he won a ten-round decision over world light heavyweight champion Gus Lesnevich in a nontitle bout. Lesnevich's handlers refused
to allow their fighter to give a title shot to Bivins. He
also defeated Hall of Famers Joey Maxim, Archie
Moore, and Ezzard Charles, though Moore and Charles
avenged their defeats multiple times in return bouts
with Bivins.

8. PACKEY MCFARLAND

Known as the "Pride of the Stockyards," Packey
McFarland went from knocking out fellow employees
at the Chicago Stockyard to becoming one of the best
professional fighters of the World War I era. A longtime
lightweight contender, he never received a title shot
from champion Battling Nelson. The two did nearly
come to blows outside the Hotel Astoria in New York
City. In his eleven-year pro career, McFarland lost only
one bout—a fifth-round stoppage to one Dusty Miller.
He did have thirty-four no-decisions, a common occur-
rence in those days after the passage of the so-called
Frawley Law. This New York law allowed ten-round
bouts but forbade decisions. The man known as the
"Chicago Flash" should have been a world champion.
Boxing historian Alexander Johnston wrote of McFarland in his book *Ten and Out! The Complete Story of
the Prize Ring in America*: "This McFarland was later
to leave an indelible mark on the lightweight division,
though he never actually won a title." He died in 1936
and was inducted into the International Boxing Hall of
Fame in 1992.

9. JOE JEANETTE

Joe Jeanette was another great African-American
heavyweight during the early part of the twentieth cen-

tury victimized by the color line. He never received a title shot from the white champions nor even from the first African-American heavyweight champion, Jack Johnson. Jeanette, however, battled Johnson numerous times before Johnson became champion. He defeated Johnson once, lost once, and fought numerous no-decisions or draws with the great fighter. Jeanette also had numerous clashes with fellow great Sam McVey.

10. SAM MCVEY

Sam McVey was another top African-American heavyweight denied a shot at the heavyweight crown because of his race. He fought many of his bouts against other greats of his race including Jack Johnson, Sam Langford, Joe Jeanette, and Harry Wills.

In fact, McVey battled Langford a whopping fifteen times and Jeanette five times. McVey died in 1921 from pneumonia.

Worst Heavyweight Challengers

Boxing fans like to see champions defend their titles against top contenders. Unfortunately, politics often prevents that from happening. Other times champions and their management desire to face an easy opponent to ensure that they hold on to their world title. The following heavyweights got a shot at the crown jewel of boxing—the world heavyweight title—even though they had less-than-glowing credentials.

1. SCOTT FRANK

A former New Jersey state heavyweight champion, Frank developed his career under Lou Duva's guidance at the Totowa Ice Arena. Duva was quoted in *The Ring* as saying, "One day in the gym he'll look like a top contender, and the next day he's not even a four round fighter." Scott qualified for his 1983 shot at Larry Holmes by receiving a nationally televised gift in the form of a draw against Renaldo Snipes. The only names of note on Frank's ledger were aging former contenders Chuck Wepner and Ron Stander. During the title bout, Holmes took target practice, landing his famed jab and right crosses at will until the fifth round when Frank clutched his right eye and then slumped to a knee, claiming he had been thumbed. Moments later, the fight was stopped.

2. JEAN-PIERRE COOPMAN

Pegged by an enterprising publicist as the "Lion of Flanders," Belgium's Coopman entered his title attempt against Muhammad Ali on February 20, 1976, with a record of 24–3. Coopman was also advertised as Belgium's heavyweight champion, even though the small European country had only a handful of licensed professional heavyweights. The challenger's cornermen provided a unique strategy for the fight, pouring champagne for Coopman between rounds. Coopman pushed forward throughout the contest eating Ali's infrequent jabs and never returning any punches of his own. At one point, Ali turned to the press and said, "You'd better pray for this guy. I'm doing my best to make a show, but he's got nothin.'" In the fifth round Ali landed a right uppercut to Coopman's head, and the challenger was counted out.

3. PETE RADEMACHER

After winning a gold medal at the 1956 Olympic Games in Melbourne, Australia, Rademacher signed to fight heavyweight champion Floyd Patterson in his very first professional fight. The unique contest between amateur and professional champions took place on August 22, 1957, in Seattle, Washington. Rademacher almost pulled off an upset when he knocked Patterson down in the second. However, the champion rose and proceeded to pummel the novice professional. He dropped Rademacher seven times and halted him in the sixth.

4. **RICHARD DUNN**

On May 24, 1976, Muhammad Ali defended his world heavyweight title against British challenger Richard Dunn in Munich, Germany. Bob Fitzsimmons had been the last British-born champion seventy-seven years earlier, and Dunn was given little chance of ending the long drought. The European champion entered the contest with a record of 33–9, and he had been stopped in eight of those losses. This was the first time Munich had hosted an international sporting event since the 1972 Olympics, when terrorists murdered seven Israeli athletes in the middle of the games. Dunn took punishment throughout the contest and went down five times as Ali stood in center ring on prime-time television, whirling his right hand like a helicopter and landing it at will on the challenger. Finally, the referee stepped in and halted the one-sided affair in the fifth round.

5. **JESSE "THE BOOGIEMAN" FERGUSON**

Jesse Ferguson began his professional boxing career with thirteen straight wins, including a win over future champion James "Buster" Douglas. But his career took a downward spiral as he lost four of his next five fights. In February 1993, Ferguson entered the ring against heavyweight prospect "Merciless" Ray Mercer as an afterthought. The bout was supposed to be a tune-up for Mercer before he battled heavyweight champion Riddick Bowe. Amazingly, Ferguson gave the performance of his career to capture a ten-round decision in a bout marred by controversy. Allegedly, Mercer tried to bribe Ferguson to drop the fight. Ferguson would have none of it and earned himself a shot at Bowe. Though losing eight of his previous fifteen bouts,

Ferguson had earned his shot at the crown in a bout widely perceived as a gross mismatch. In May 1993, Ferguson and his handlers chanted "Bowe Must Go" in their walk to the ring. Unfortunately, the prognosticators were correct, as Ferguson was in way over his head. Bowe pounded him out in two rounds. Ferguson retired in 1999 with a record of 26–18.

6. LEE OMA

Chicago's Lee Oma was a mediocre heavyweight who was kayoed sixteen times in his career, including four straight and seven total kayo losses in 1941 alone. His inept performances even led him to be suspended, and he did not fight again until 1943. Oma did manage to turn his career around in later years. His big break came when he upset contender Bob Satterfield in 1950 to win a ten-round decision. That fight landed him a shot at world champion Ezzard Charles. Though Oma entered the ring with a record of 62–26–4, he gave a surprisingly decent account of himself, lasting until the tenth round. He retired from the ring after his title loss.

7. RON STANDER

Stander, known as the "Council Bluffs Butcher," won twenty-one of his first twenty-two bouts against limited opposition fighting in Midwest hinterlands such as Elgin, Illinois, and Waterloo, Iowa. However, he did defeat vaunted puncher Earnie Shavers in 1970. On May 5, 1972, in Omaha, Nebraska, Stander challenged heavyweight champion "Smokin" Joe Frazier for the world title. Stander's wife accurately summed up her husband's chances, telling the press, "It's like entering a Volkswagen in the Indianapolis 500." Stander absorbed tremendous punishment from Frazier until the referee mercifully halted the contest after five rounds. After the shot at Frazier, Stander spent the rest of his career as a journeyman boxer, losing twenty-one more fights, many to very limited opposition.

8. JACK ROPER

Roper was heavyweight great Joe Louis's sixth title challenger. At age thirty-six, Roper was considered over the hill and a soft touch for the Brown Bomber. The bout was staged in Los Angeles and was California's first heavyweight title fight in thirty years. Roper's record was unverifiable, but it was thought to be less than sparkling to say the least. Roper came out on the attack first, winging left hooks and even catching Louis early in the first round. But the champion quickly rectified matters, winning in the first round.

9. LORENZO ZANON

Italy's Lorenzo Zanon did nothing to deserve a shot at the world heavyweight title, but in the boxing world of alphabet soup he received his shot against champion Larry Holmes in February 1980. Previously, Zanon had suffered kayo losses to Jerry Quarry, Ken Norton, and someone named Dante Cane. His only claims to fame were two decision victories over an equally unqualified Alfredo Evangelista. The glass-jawed Zanon predictably proved to be no match for Holmes, who stopped him in the sixth round.

10. TERRY DANIELS

Terry Daniels was a college student and football player at Southern Methodist University who decided to try professional boxing in 1969. He seemed like an odd candidate for a professional boxing career, since he was less than a semester away from graduating and was the son of a millionaire. Daniels challenged "Smokin" Joe Frazier on January 15, 1972, in New Orleans. Daniels put up a game effort but bounced off the canvas several times on his way to a fourth-round defeat. Daniels resumed his career after the Frazier fight but went a dismal 5–25 after his title shot.

Hapless Heavyweights

M ost fighters are not champions, contenders, or even prospects. They are fighters who build or pad the records of other fighters. They fight in order to make a few hundred bucks here and there. If they are lucky, they may nab a higher purse every now and then. The following fighters have padded the records of many good heavyweights through the years.

1. KEN BENTLEY

Ken Bentley of Chattanooga, Tennessee, fought professionally from 1975 to 2001. Fighting well into his forties, Bentley labored his way to a record of 9–94–1, losing his last eighteen bouts. In many of his fights, he would do little more than hold and back into a crouching position on the ropes in an attempt to avoid punishment. His defense-mindedness enabled him to go the distance with many fighters, including Shannon Briggs and Carlos "Sugar" DeLeon. Bentley's skills were so deficient that he even lost to Frankie Hines and Roy Bedwell, two other fighters on this list.

2. FRANKIE HINES

Frankie Hines of Shelby, North Carolina, began his professional career as a middleweight in 1980. Over the years, Hines put on weight ostensibly to get more fights and perhaps more money. Hines will often throw fewer than ten punches a round and focus solely on defense, which for him consists of an odd backpedaling gait. At the end of 2002, his record was an abysmal 17–119–5. But the year closed on a high note for the affable Hines, as he won his next-to-last fight of 2002—a four-round decision over Jeff Holcomb.

3. JAMES HOLLY

James Holly is a heavyweight from Ashtabula, Ohio—a locale known for being home to so many inept boxers that the Association of Boxing Commissioners sent out an alert list on Ashtabula fighters to different state commissioners. Holly fought from 1983 to 2000. Once he fought under the name James Robinson (his son's name), and later in the week he used his real name in another bout. Though he actually began his career by winning two of his first three fights, he ended up at 5–63. Incredibly, Holly was stopped in all sixty-three of his losses. He lost more than twenty-five bouts by first-round knockouts.

4. GEORGE HARRIS

George Harris was a heavyweight from Ashtabula, Ohio, who fought from 1991 to 1999, compiling a record of 2–37. He failed to reach the final bell in thirty-five of his thirty-seven losses. Harris usually lost by kayo in the first or second round, including a 1998 first-round loss to former world champion Greg Page.

5. **BRIAN YATES**

Brian "B-52" Yates from Indianapolis, Indiana, fought from 1992 until 2001, tallying an unenviable record of 13–85–3. Yates's chief (and perhaps only) claim to fame is that he ended former heavyweight contender Earnie Shavers's comeback in 1995 with a second-round stoppage of the fifty-two-year-old Shavers. Yates actually possesses decent power and a sturdy chin. Many times he performed just hard enough to lose.

6. **DANNY WOFFORD**

A potbellied heavyweight from Spartanburg, South Carolina, Danny Wofford actually began his career promisingly enough as a super middleweight in 1987. In his first nine fights, Wofford went 7–1–1. However, his career began to decline as he gained weight to obtain more fights and larger purses, and, by October 2003, his record stood at 17–98–2. Wofford normally engages more in clowning tactics, such as wiggling his big belly at his opponent, rather than actual boxing. Wofford is a durable opponent who has gone the distance with talented boxers such as Pinklon Thomas, Robert Daniels, Shannon Briggs, Maurice Harris, and James Warring.

7. **ROY BEDWELL**

Roy Bedwell of Jackson, Tennessee, began his professional boxing career in 1986 as a super middleweight. He won his first five bouts but quickly deteriorated into a blown-up heavyweight. By October 2003, Bedwell's record stood at 15–71–1, and he even lost by kayo to middleweight Brad Austin in 2001. Bedwell has lost his last nineteen bouts, though he did go the four-round distance with crowd favorite Eric Esch, better known as Butterbean or the "King of the Four-Rounders."

8. JAMES WILDER

James Wilder was a heavyweight from Milwaukee, Wisconsin, who fought from 1982 to 1998, compiling a terrible tally of 3–53–1. His only claim to fame was a 1993 win over an aging Leon Spinks, the former heavyweight champion of the world, in Davenport, Iowa. Unlike many of his colleagues on this list, Wilder usually went the distance in a losing cause.

9. STAN JOHNSON

Stan Johnson is a heavyweight from Milwaukee, Wisconsin, who began his professional boxing career in 1982. He is better known as a handler who provides "opponents" who lose in local club fights. Johnson's full record is hard to obtain because he fought under a veritable phonebook of aliases, including Stanley Wright and Jack Jackson. Jake Hall, Indiana boxing commissioner, says that Johnson even fought in his state using his son's name, Stanley Johnson.

10. JIM WISNIEWSKI

Jim "Watermelon Man" Wisniewski from Wisconsin compiled a record of 4–29 in a career running from 1986 to 1998. Wisniewski was a colorfully inept fighter with little skill who earned his nickname by winning a watermelon-eating contest. In the ring, Wisniewski ate his share of punches. In 1998, he lost in the first round to Mike Fitzgerald, the coauthor of this book.

The Journeyman/ Survivors

In boxing, you have champions, contenders, and prospects on one side. Then you have journeymen, trial horses, and outright tomato cans on the other. Most prospects feast on journeymen to build their records and confidence before they test their abilities against better fighters. Some fighters are relegated forever to the status of journeyman. They often pride themselves on lasting until the final bell, frustrating a would-be prospect's attempt at a knockout. Some journeymen have even acquired a measure of fame for their numerous losses. For example, Bruce "The Mouse" Strauss's ring ineptness was chronicled in a *Sports Illustrated* profile and a 1996 movie. The following is a list of boxing's staunchest journeymen.

1. JOE GRIM

Born Saverio Giannone in Italy, Joe Grim moved with his family to America. He is a legend in boxing history thanks to his uncanny ability to absorb punishment, which led him to be labeled "The Human Punching Bag," "The Iron Man," and the "Indian Rubber Man." When he finished a fight, Grim would yell to the crowd:

"I am Joe Grim! I fear no man on earth!" Even heavy-weight champions Jack Johnson and Bob Fitzsim-mons couldn't keep him down on the canvas for a ten-count. Not surprisingly, Grim finished his life in an insane asylum.

2. REGGIE STRICKLAND

The incomparable Reggie Strickland, who has per-formed under several aliases including Reggie Buse and Reggie Raglin, has fought more than 330 bouts, losing 252. He has probably lost more bouts than any boxer in history. But Strickland, who goes by the nick-name of "Nightlife," actually possesses some decent defensive skills. Some boxing experts even suggest he could have been a contender if he had trained properly. Most speculate that he simply realized he could make more money losing a fight every week or so.

3. ARNOLD "KID" SHEPPARD

A former welterweight from Cardiff, Wales, Arnold "Kid" Sheppard fought 276 bouts between 1926 and 1939. His record was 96–154–36. He often fought hurt and on very short notice. Most of his bouts went the distance.

4. DONNIE PENELTON

Donnie Penelton, known as the "Spoiler" or the "Black Battle Cat," has made a career out of going the dis-tance and doing just enough to lose. Penelton, a cousin of former world champion Gerald McClellan, possesses good boxing skills but often focuses strictly on defense. He has faced a who's who of rising prospects including Derrick Harmon, Thomas Ulrich, Rydell Booker, Jose Spearman, Jonathan Corn, and Jason Robinson. His record is 13–141–4. He holds two decision wins over Reggie Strickland.

5. GEORGE "SCRAP IRON" JOHNSON

Journeyman heavyweight George "Scrap Iron" Johnson fought from 1958 to 1975 against many top heavyweight contenders. The portly Johnson, who stood only 5′9″, rarely took a backward step. Though he had more losses than wins (20–24–5), he gave the fans and his opponents their money's worth. He went the ten-round distance with Jerry Quarry, Joe Bugner, Eddie Machen, and Joe Frazier. He lasted seven rounds with the two most feared heavyweights of their day, Sonny Liston and George Foreman. In 2002, Johnson was given an Award of Merit by the World Boxing Hall of Fame.

6. TEDDY WORTH

Lightweight Teddy Worth from the province of New Brunswick, in Canada, has a record of 9–46–4. In a pro career that began in 1995, he has been stopped in only three of his forty-six losses. Worth has shown his worthy chin and the ability to absorb a tremendous amount of punishment.

7. MANUEL SANTIAGO

Manuel (or Manny) Santiago, nicknamed "Cold Sweat," was a lightweight from Puerto Rico who was often used as a stepping-stone for young prospects. He fought from 1987 to 1998. Though his record was only 6–47, he was stopped only five times. The other forty-two losses were on points.

8. ANGELO SIMPSON

Angelo Simpson is a cruiserweight from Montgomery, Alabama, with a record of 6–36–2. Though he sports

Scott Romer

With close to 150 losses against only 14 wins,
Donnie Penelton is a favorite opponent of up-and-comers
looking to increase their win total.

an unflattering record, Simpson has never been stopped. The only time he failed to go the distance was a seventh-round disqualification in 1998 to contender Mohammed Ben Guesmia. He turned pro in 1994 and won his first four bouts before the tailspin began.

9. BENJI SINGLETON

Benji Singleton, nicknamed "Bad News," often thwarts prospects who want to pad their knockout totals at his expense. This junior middleweight from Charlotte, North Carolina, will employ his awkward defensive style to usually go the distance. He has faced many top fighters in his career including former world junior middleweight champion Laurent Boudaini. He began his career in 1993, and his record stands at 25–92–4.

10. JIM KACZMAREK

Lanky welterweight Jim Kaczmarek possesses little boxing skill. His record of 21–80–4 attests to his lack of ability. But the awkward Kaczmarek has proven to be a difficult opponent to knock out, as he has been stopped only once in his last twenty-six defeats. He began his pro career in 1988, and his last recorded bout was in 2000.

Controversial Decisions

Boxing has been plagued with controversial decisions since its infancy. Scoring a fight is a subjective proposition, and sometimes outside considerations have been known to intrude. In the early part of the twentieth century, a single referee scored a bout. Sometimes, the referee was seen as less than impartial. For instance, in 1916, referee Billy Rocap scored the title bout between Kid Williams and Pete Herman a draw; even though most ringside observers thought Herman was the clear winner. Rocap and Williams were friends. In the 1920s, it became common for judges to score a fight. In other jurisdictions, two judges and referee would score the bout. Today, three judges sitting at ringside score fights based on four basic criteria—clean punching, effective aggression, ring generalship, and defense.

Most bad decisions occur at the club-fight level when a hometown fighter faces an imported opponent. The crowd roars its support for the hometown guy, which can have an effect on fight judges who live there, too. But there have been plenty of high-profile bad decisions and outright robberies. The following is a list of ten such controversial decisions.

1. ALFREDO ESCALERA W15 TYRONE EVERETT (November 30, 1976, Philadelphia, Pennsylvania)

Boxing experts consistently describe this decision as corrupt and perhaps the worst of all time. Most ringside observers believe that Everett, a southpaw, won at least ten of the fifteen rounds. Harold Lederman, HBO's unofficial boxing expert and longtime world class judge, ranked the fight in an interview on Fightnews.com as easily the worst and most "incredibly strange" decision he has ever seen. Lederman, too, believes Everett won at least ten of the fifteen rounds.

Ironically, Everett lost the bout even though the event was held in his hometown of Philadelphia, Pennsylvania. Escalera would go on to lose two classic bouts with the great Alexis Arguello in 1978 and 1979. Unfortunately, Everett never got a rematch with Escalera. He was shot and killed shortly before the rematch was to take place. The supposed "loss" to Escalera was the only defeat of Everett's career.

2. LENNOX LEWIS D15 EVANDER HOLYFIELD (March 13, 1999, New York, New York)

It might seem strange to rank a draw as one of the worst decisions of all time, but the magnitude of the bout and Lewis's dominance in it dictate otherwise. Simply stated, Lewis put on a boxing clinic, winning nine of the twelve rounds on many people's scorecards—except for the three judges' cards. Judge Eugenia Williams actually scored the bout 115–113 for Holyfield in one of the most heavily criticized scorecards of all time. The

draw led to a litany of proposed federal and state legis-
lation. The New York legislature considered measures
such as open scoring and fighting an extra round in the
case of a draw. Fortunately, the two champions fought
a rematch, and Lewis won a unanimous decision in a
bout that was actually closer than their first fight.

3. JOSE LUIS RAMIREZ W12 PERNELL WHITAKER (March 12, 1988, Paris, France)

Judges from Brazil and France thwarted Pernell "Sweet
Pea" Whitaker's first attempt at a lightweight world title.
Most shrewd observers believed that Whitaker won at
least eight of the twelve rounds with his superior boxing
skills and defensive wizardry. However, Judges Newton
Campos of Brazil and Louis Michel of France somehow
deemed champion Jose Luis Ramirez the winner.

Shelly Finkel, Whitaker's manager, was outraged at
the decision and alleged collusion between promoter
Don King and WBC president Jose Sulaiman. He ac-
cused the two of conspiring to fix the fight. The WBC
fired back with a lawsuit, claiming that Finkel and Whitaker trainer Lou Duva had defamed the organization
with their charges of a fixed fight. Whitaker was
awarded a rematch and defeated Ramirez easily the
following year.

4. MIKE MCTIGUE W10 TIGER FLOWERS (December 23, 1925, New York, New York)

This bout featured popular Irish light heavyweight Mike
McTigue against Theodore "Tiger" Flowers, the first
African-American to win the world middleweight crown
and the first African-American to win a world title after
the legendary Jack Johnson. This bout was judged by
officials who had never before judged professional

fights, including department store owner Bernard Gimbel and banker Peter J. Brady. Nearly every expert thought Flowers, nicknamed "The Georgia Deacon," won the fight, but the celebrity judges gave the decision to McTigue.

The boxing public obviously thought Flowers deserved the decision because his performance earned him—not McTigue—a title shot against fellow future Hall of Famer Harry Greb, which he won. In 1927, Flowers had surgery to remove scar tissue around his eyes. He died four days later from complications of the surgery. Coincidentally, Greb had died during a similar procedure a year earlier.

5.   MICKEY WALKER W10 TIGER FLOWERS
(December 3, 1926, Chicago, Illinois)

Once again, "The Georgia Deacon" was robbed in the month of December—this time at the Chicago Coliseum. Flowers defended his world middleweight crown against fellow future Hall of Famer Mickey "The Toy Bulldog" Walker, former world welterweight champion.

The two judges split 1–1 in favor of each fighter, but referee Benny Yanger, serving as the third judge, sided with Walker. Most ringside experts believed that Flowers had given Walker a boxing lesson in most of the rounds. *The Boxing Register International Hall of Fame Official Record Book* reads: "Flowers lost his title to Mickey Walker in Chicago, even though Flowers had dominated the fight. The judges' questionable decision was investigated by the Illinois State Athletic Commission, but Walker still held the title." Flowers doggedly pursued a rematch with Walker, but his quest was cut short by his tragic death from surgical complications.

6. LUPE PINTOR W15 CARLOS ZARATE
(June 3, 1979, Las Vegas, Nevada)

Boxing experts smelled a rat when Mexican warrior Carlos Zarate and Lupe Pintor fought for the WBC bantamweight crown. Arturo Hernandez of Mexico City managed both fighters. The oddest thing about the scoring in this bout was the extreme disparity between the judge who voted for Zarate and the two who scored it for Pintor. The latter both scored the bout 143–142 for Pintor. But Bob Martin had the bout 145–133 for Zarate. The Associated Press also had Zarate winning by a whopping nine points.

Longtime boxing writer Royce Feour wrote in the *Las Vegas Review-Journal* in a December 1999 column: "I still remember the shocked look on Pintor's face when he was announced as the winner." After the controversial loss, Zarate petitioned the World Boxing Council to reverse the decision. President Jose Sulaiman agreed the decision was incorrect but refused to change it.

7. JAMES TONEY W12 DAVE TIBERI
(February 8, 1992, Atlantic City, New Jersey)

James "Lights Out" Toney was considered one of the best pound-for-pound boxers in the early 1990s. It was expected that he would have an easy time with the unheralded Dave Tiberi of Delaware. But Tiberi took the fight to Toney and should have captured the crown, according to many ringside observers.

One judge scored the bout 117–111 for Tiberi, but the other two scored it 115–112 and 115–111 for Toney. ABC boxing analyst Alex Wallau was so incensed after the verdict that he said Tiberi won the crown but "a couple of incompetent people at ringside robbed him of that." Donald Trump, who owned the casino where the fight was held, called the result the worst he had ever seen. The decision against his constituent so outraged Senator William Roth of Delaware that he spearheaded a U.S. Senate investigation into the sport of boxing.

Tiberi never fought again. His career was described in a biography entitled *Tiberi: The Uncrowned Champion.* For his part, James Toney is still a top-rated fighter, winning a world cruiserweight title in April 2003.

8. SHANNON BRIGGS W12 GEORGE FOREMAN (November 22, 1997, Atlantic City, New Jersey)

This bout featured the enigmatic and erratic Shannon Briggs versus the still formidable forty-eight-year-old George Foreman. Foreman appeared to control the action with his punishing jab. He was the aggressor, dictating the pace for most of the fight. Compubox's Punchstat numbers had Foreman landing nearly sixty more punches. He also appeared to land the harder blows. Yet one judge scored the bout even at 114–114, but the two other judges scored it 116–112 and an incomprehensible 117–111 for Briggs. Foreman's HBO colleagues Jim Lampley, Larry Merchant, and Harold Lederman were stunned by the verdict, as were most viewers. It was a stinker.

9. JOE LOUIS W15 JERSEY JOE WALCOTT (December 5, 1947, New York, New York)

Heavyweight king Joe Louis was mowing through the division, kayoing a series of opponents in what some dubbed the "Bum of the Month" tour. His next opponent was also considered overmatched—an at-least thirty-three-year-old Jersey Joe Walcott (some say Walcott was much older). The fight was considered such a mismatch that it was originally scheduled as a nontitle bout. Walcott was a twenty-to-one underdog. But that night in Madison Square Garden, many ringside observers believed Jersey Joe beat Louis. Walcott dropped Louis twice, in the first and fourth rounds with picture-perfect right hands both times. The clever ring tactician simply appeared to outbox the champion. Referee Rudy Goldstein saw it that way, voting for Walcott. However, the two ringside judges sided with Louis.

Boxing historian Bert Sugar wrote in his 1982 book *100 Years of Boxing*: "A disheartened Louis, believing he had lost, started to leave the ring before the decision was announced. Restrained by cooler heads, he was rewarded with a split decision for his efforts. For the first time in his career, Joe heard the crowd boo him." Louis would redeem himself in June 1948 with an eleventh-round stoppage of Walcott. Walcott would go on to greater glory when he captured the world championship by defeating Ezzard Charles in July 1951.

10. ULTIMINIO "SUGAR" RAMOS W15 FLOYD ROBERTSON (May 9, 1964, Accra, Ghana)

In 1964, Ultiminio "Sugar" Ramos was the popular world featherweight champion. He was expected to brawl his way past Robertson as he had most of his other opponents. But the heavy-fisted Ramos got all he wanted and more from Robertson in the latter's homeland of Ghana.

Herbert Goldman listed this in his top-ten all-time worst decisions in a 1986 *Ring* magazine article, writing that "there was almost an international incident over this one." Robertson floored Ramos twice but still did not win the decision. The Ghana Boxing Authority later called the bout a no-contest and then declared Robertson the winner. However, the World Boxing Association said the judges' verdict stood, and Ramos retained the title. Apparently, the Robertson fight took a lot out of Ramos, for in his very next fight he lost his crown to Vincente Saldivar. Robertson got another crack at a world title in 1966, but Saldivar stopped him in the second round.

Dirty Fighters

These fighters had the reputation of doing anything they could to win a fight, be it fair or foul.

1. AMOS SMITH

Amos Smith, better known as Mysterious Billy Smith, was born in either Maine or Canada. He held the welterweight championship from 1898 to 1900. Smith lost an amazing eleven bouts by disqualification, including fights to Charles "Kid" McCoy, Jim Ryan, Tommy Ryan (for biting), and Charles Johnson. In 1900 alone, he lost four bouts on fouls, including a championship to James "Rube" Ferns. Ring historian William Schutte wrote a book entitled *Mysterious Billy Smith: The Dirtiest Fighter of All Time.*

2. FRITZIE ZIVIC

Pittsburgh's Fritzie Zivic, known as the "Croat Comet," is considered one of the dirtiest fighters of all time. He had a penchant for low blows, wiping his laces to aggravate cuts, and other illegal tactics. The great Henry Armstrong, who lost twice to Zivic, said of him to author Peter Heller in *In This Corner: Forty World Champi-*

ons Tell Their Stories: "He was just a nasty fighter, just a foul fighter. He did everything foul . . ." Zivic, who held the world welterweight championship, lost sixty-five bouts in his career but, amazingly, never lost a fight by disqualification.

3. HARRY GREB

Harry Greb, the "Pittsburgh Windmill," was one of the greatest middleweight champions of all time, holding the championship from 1923 to 1926. He was also one of the dirtiest fighters. He used his roughhouse tactics to hand the great Gene Tunney the only defeat of his professional career. Tunney called Greb easily the dirtiest fighter he ever faced in the ring. Greb was particularly adept at using his elbows, head, and even knees as weapons. He frequently threw rabbit punches, hitting opponents on the back of their head and neck.

4. TONY GALENTO

Former potbellied bartender Tony "Two Ton" Galento brawled his way to a shot at world heavyweight champion Joe Louis. "Who is Queensberry?" he reportedly replied when questioned about his seeming disregard for the rules of modern boxing laid down by the Marquis of Queensberry in the nineteenth century. Galento showed no regard for rules as he butted, gouged, and bit opponents in his memorable career. Though he possessed little boxing skill, Galento pummeled his way to more than seventy wins in his professional career. Surprisingly, he lost only one fight by disqualification in his colorful career.

5. EUSEBIO PEDROZA

Eusebio Pedroza held the WBA world featherweight title from 1978 to 1985, defending it an amazing nineteen times. Even though he was tall (5'9") for a feather-weight, Pedroza was adept at inside fighting. He often resorted to dirty tactics in his championship reign. In 1982, he captured a close decision over Juan LaPorte. His low blows and illegal kidney punches led the referee to deduct two points from him during the bout. LaPorte called Pedroza "the dirtiest fighter I ever fought."

6. MIKE TYSON

Mike Tyson, the youngest man to ever win the world heavyweight title, merits inclusion on this list for his egregious conduct during his second fight with Evander Holyfield. Whether he was upset by Holyfield's head butts or simply was seeking to escape from a probable beating, Tyson committed an unpardonable sin in November 1997. Twice he bit Holyfield's ear, the first time taking off a piece of the champion's ear. Later, Tyson earned a no-contest for hitting Orlin Norris after the bell. He also appeared to be trying to break the arm of opponent Francois Botha during a clinch in the opening round of their fight.

7. ANDREW GOLOTA

Polish heavyweight Andrew Golota, sometimes referred to disparagingly as the "Foul Pole," has made a career out of bizarre behavior in and out of the ring. His foul tactics in the ring including biting Samson P'ouha on the shoulder and two disqualifications for repeated low blows against former world heavyweight champion Riddick Bowe. The low blows against Bowe were particularly inexplicable, as Golota was ahead on the scorecards in each fight.

8. ANDRE ROUTIS

Frenchman Andre Routis won the world featherweight championship in 1928. He was involved in an amazing number of bouts that ended in disqualification. He lost at least five bouts by disqualification, including bouts to Jackie "Kid" Berg and Joe Salas. He also won numerous bouts by disqualification. Most of Routis's disqualifications were for low blows.

9. ROBERTO DURAN

Roberto Duran was one of the greatest fighters of all time, winning world championships from lightweight to middleweight in a career that spanned five decades. At lightweight he was an absolute terror, punishing opponents with ruthless assaults that often included blows from his elbow and head. He roughed up Ken Buchanan with a low blow during their title fight and used roughhouse tactics to hand Sugar Ray Leonard his first professional defeat.

10. EVANDER HOLYFIELD

While it may seem somewhat sacrilegious, Evander Holyfield deserves mention on this list based on what many of his opponents have said. Holyfield has made effective use of his head as a weapon in many of his bouts. George Foreman once said Holyfield was the dirtiest fighter he ever faced. Likewise, fellow Holyfield opponents Mike Tyson, Lennox Lewis, John Ruiz, and Hasim Rahman all complained about Evander's dirty tactics, primarily his frequent head butts.

Prison Boxers

Unfortunately, many boxers have known the penal system on a firsthand basis. Perhaps it is the rough-and-tumble nature of the sport that attracts many with a hardcore edge. Perhaps boxing simply affords a way out for tough kids. Whatever the case, many boxers have picked up the sport of boxing in some type of penal institution—be it a reform school or full-fledged gray-bar hotel.

Some boxers have literally gone from rags to riches, trading a jail cell for a championship kingdom. Tragically, other boxers have reverted back to their bad ways and returned to prison. Though their experiences are vastly different, all of the following boxers, at one time or another, spent time in a penal institution.

1. SONNY LISTON

Born in the rural South in a family with twenty-three siblings, Charles "Sonny" Liston learned to fight to survive. Liston learned to box in the Missouri State Penitentiary when he was serving time for armed robbery. He began boxing in a program run by the prison chaplain. Liston learned his lessons well and became a hated but great heavyweight champion of the world who dominated the division with his menacing glare and devastating power—until he faced Cassius Clay. When reigning champion Floyd Patterson finally gave Liston a title shot in 1962, Liston destroyed him in one round. He also kayoed Patterson in one round in their 1963 rematch. After consecutive losses to Cassius Clay/Muhammad Ali, Liston won fourteen fights in a row before a surprise kayo loss to Leotis Martin in a fight Liston was winning. He died under mysterious circumstances in 1970. The stated cause of death was a drug overdose, but questions are still raised about his death, with some calling it murder.

2. JAMES SCOTT

James Scott was a top-ranked light heavyweight contender in the late 1970s and early 1980s who fought many bouts while an inmate at Rahway State Prison in New Jersey. He fought there because he was serving time for armed robbery and later murder. Scott fought his first eleven pro bouts in Miami Beach, Florida, winning them all. Then he began serving time in Rahway. Amazingly, he was allowed to fight eleven times in Rahway State Prison against several top contenders. At Rahway, he defeated top fighters such as Eddie Mustafa Muhammad, Yaqui Lopez, Jerry Celestine, and Richie Kates. His last fight was a ten-round decision loss to future champion Dwight Braxton (who would change his name to Dwight Muhammad Qawi). A new warden at Rahway refused to allow any more bouts at the prison. Scott's record was 19–2–1. He currently is serving a life sentence at South Woods State Prison in Bridgeton, New Jersey.

3. MIKE TYSON

Michael Gerard Tyson grew up on the mean streets of Brownsville, New York. His wild behavior led him to Tryon Reform School in Johnstown, New York. It was there that aging trainer Cus D'Amato discovered him. The rest, as they say, is history. Tyson stormed to the world heavyweight title at age twenty and unified the titles before he was twenty-two. Unfortunately, he has not been able to avoid the penal system as an adult. He served three and a half years in an Indiana prison for rape and has had numerous other brushes with the law. He is still a contender in the heavyweight division, hoping to reclaim past glory.

4. ARCHIE MOORE

The ageless Archie Moore, who fought until he was fifty-four, served two years of his early life in reform school in St. Louis, Missouri. It was there that Moore learned how to box and made the decision to turn his life around after his release. He joined the Civilian Conservation Corps and became an amateur boxer. He began his pro boxing career in 1936 and retired after bouts with Cassius Clay and Mike DiBiase. Known for his incredible longevity, Moore is also credited with more knockouts than any fighter in professional boxing history.

5. RON LYLE

Ron Lyle was a top heavyweight contender for much of the 1970s known for his title loss to Muhammad Ali and his classic war with George Foreman. Lyle learned to box while serving seven and a half years in prison on a second-degree murder conviction. He held victories over Oscar Bonavena, Buster Mathis, Earnie Shavers, Joe Bugner, and Jimmy Ellis. Lyle retired in 1980. He returned to the ring in his fifties in 1995, probably inspired by his old foe Foreman, and won four straight bouts.

6. FLOYD CUMMINGS

Floyd "Jumbo" Cummings was a one-time fringe heavyweight contender who learned boxing while serving a murder sentence at an Illinois state correctional facility. Cummings is best known for foiling former world champ Joe Frazier's ill-fated comeback in December 1981. The bout was scored a draw, though most ringside observers felt Cummings deserved the nod. Cummings began his career with fourteen straight wins. He retired in 1983 after his fifth straight loss with a record of 15–6–1. He is now serving a life sentence in an Illinois prison.

7. CLIFFORD ETIENNE

Clifford Etienne, known as the "Black Rhino," is a heavyweight contender with an exciting style and suspect chin. Etienne learned to box in a Louisiana prison program where he served ten years in two different prisons from 1988 to 1998 on an armed robbery conviction. He became the state prison boxing champ and, upon his release, embarked on his pro career. He has compiled a record of 24–2–1, but in February 2003 lasted only forty-nine seconds with Mike Tyson.

8. JULIAN LETTERLOUGH

Nicknamed "Mr. KO," light heavyweight Julian Letterlough thrills fight fans with his tremendous punching power. But Letterlough was not always in the limelight.

He served seven years in a Pennsylvania state prison for aggravated assault where he learned to box in prison from an inmate named Tyrone Payne. He moved up in weight to challenge IBF world cruiserweight champ Vassili Jirov in September 2001. He has a record of 19–5–2 with seventeen kayoes.

9. MICHAEL BENNETT

Michael Bennett represented the United States in the 2000 Olympic Games in Sydney, Australia, in the heavyweight division. Bennett was twenty-nine when he represented his country. He was older than most amateurs because he spent seven years of an original sentence of more than twenty years in jail for armed

Chris Cozzone

Michael Bennett, shown here after a kayo of Donald Macon, learned how to box while serving prison time for armed robbery and went on to represent the United States in the Olympics before turning pro.

robbery. He learned to box in prison from other inmates. When he was released he joined Garfield Park Gym in Chicago and became a celebrated amateur. After the Olympics, Bennett turned professional. He has a record of 10–4 with eight kayoes.

10. **KASSAN SAXTON**

Kassan Saxton was an undefeated heavyweight prospect from New Jersey who was 5–0. He was arrested in October 1995 for second-degree murder of a United New York, Inc. insurance executive. Saxton had been previously convicted of manslaughter in 1982 and served eleven years before being paroled in 1993. Saxton became an undefeated amateur boxer, going 58–0 while serving his sentence and winning eight New Jersey state prison championships.

Cop Boxers

Certainly not all boxers have run afoul of the law. In fact, many pugilists have served on the other side of the law as police officers, sheriff deputies, and prison guards. The following boxers all served as law enforcement officials either during or after their careers.

1. JERSEY JOE WALCOTT

Born Arnold Cream, Jersey Joe Walcott was a truly great fighter who captured the world heavyweight title in 1951 with a seventh-round stoppage of rival Ezzard Charles. In 1947, he lost a controversial fifteen-round decision to the great Joe Louis, a fight that even Louis thought he had lost. Walcott lost the title via a spectacular thirteenth-round kayo at the hands of Rocky Marciano. Walcott was a success outside of the ring as well. In 1972, he became sheriff of Camden, New Jersey, and later became chairman of the New Jersey State Athletic Commission.

2. TOMMY GIBBONS

Tommy Gibbons of St. Paul, Minnesota, fought as a welterweight on up to heavyweight in his fourteen-year

Hall of Fame career. In the biggest fight of his career, he lost a fifteen-round decision to the great Jack Dempsey for the world heavyweight title in Shelby, Montana, in 1923. He retired after losing to Gene Tunney, finishing with a record of 57–4–1 with forty-three no-decisions. Upon retirement, he served four terms as sheriff of St. Paul.

3. BOB FOSTER

Bob Foster of Albuquerque, New Mexico, was one of the greatest light heavyweight champions of all time. He dominated the division in the late 1960s and early 1970s, making fourteen title defenses. He won the title with a vicious fourth-round knockout over Dick Tiger and retired as champion in 1974. Foster moved up in weight to challenge Joe Frazier for the heavyweight crown but was felled in two rounds. He also lost to Muhammad Ali in a 1972 bout. Upon retirement, Foster began a lengthy career in law enforcement.

4. JIMMY PERRIN

Born James Raymond LaCava, Jimmy Perrin was a top featherweight in the 1930s and early 1940s from New Orleans, Louisiana. A member of the 1932 Olympic team, Perrin turned professional and defeated top fighters such as Hall of Famer Sixto Escobar, Joey Archibald, and Bobby Ruffin. His home state of Louisiana recognized him as world featherweight champion after he defeated Ruffin over fifteen rounds in New Orleans. After his career, Perrin became a New Orleans police officer and, later, a member of the Louisiana Boxing Commission.

5. **PHIL ZWICK**

Nicknamed "The Wisconsin Flash," Phil Zwick was a top featherweight boxer from Kaukauna, Wisconsin. He lost a bid for the National Boxing Association (NBA) featherweight championship against champion Petey Scalzo in Milwaukee, Wisconsin, on May 19, 1941. Scalzo was awarded a decision over Zwick, but the Wisconsin Boxing Commission overruled the verdict six days later and called the fight a draw. After retiring from boxing following 250 pro fights, Zwick moved to Vallejo, California, and went to work for the local police department as an officer in the fingerprint department.

6. **SAM HILL**

Nicknamed "The Fighting Policeman," Sam Hill is a St. Louis–based police officer who moonlights as a super middleweight boxing contender. He surprised the boxing world in November 2001 with a ninth-round stoppage of former Olympic gold medalist and professional world champion David Reid. He has compiled a record of 15–5–1 with one no-contest. He has lost his last three bouts, including one to 2000 Olympian Jermain Taylor.

7. **RICHARD FRAZIER**

Richard Frazier is a New York City police officer from the twenty-sixth precinct who earned a measure of fame in the boxing world in January 1999 when he fought Roy Jones Jr. for the world light heavyweight title. The thirty-nine-year-old Frazier stepped into the ring as a huge underdog against the talented Jones. Jones stopped Frazier in the second round, and Frazier has never fought again as a professional. He retired with a record of 18–4–1.

8. TUNNEY HUNSAKER

Tunney Hunsaker was the police chief of Fayetteville, West Virginia, in 1960 when he faced a young fighter making his pro debut—Cassius Marcellus Clay. Hunsaker entered the ring with a respectable record of 17–8, but he was no match for Clay's superior hand and foot speed. Clay, who later changed his name to Muhammad Ali and became the most recognizable athlete in the world, won a unanimous six-round decision over Hunsaker in Louisville's Freedom Hall. Hunsaker considered it a great honor to be the first fighter that Ali ever faced in his professional career.

9. DICK WIPPERMAN

Dick Wipperman was a Buffalo-based, journeyman heavyweight from the 1960s who fought main events on two cards at the boxing mecca Madison Square Garden. Wipperman lost both fights—a ten-round decision to Oscar Bonavena and a kayo at the hands of future world champion "Smokin" Joe Frazier. He also lost to contenders Henry Cooper and George Chuvalo. Wipperman has been a cop in a suburb of Buffalo for more than thirty years. Dick Wipperman fought all comers and was never afraid of a tough opponent. His manager was also in the process of negotiating a fight with Sonny Liston when Dick decided to retire in 1967 after being knocked out in the second round by Bob Felstein.

10. KEN ATKINS

Ken "The Bull" Atkins was a light heavyweight who fought in the early 1990s, compiling a record of 29–4 fighting in his home state of Tennessee. In 1993, he

Patricia Halstead Hunsaker

Tunney Hunsaker was the debut opponent for Cassius Clay and lost a unanimous six-round decision to the future Muhammad Ali.

won the World Boxing Federation (WBF) light heavy-weight title. In a 1990 bout in Hawaii, Atkins lost in the third round on cuts to the great Thomas "Hitman" Hearns. The stocky Atkins was a tough customer who could take a punch. "He was the toughest and most courageous fighter I ever had," says Kerry Pharr, his manager/trainer. Atkins became a police officer in his hometown of Smyrna, Tennessee, before he turned professional. He remains a police officer.

Worst Ring Tragedies

Boxing fans believe that the sport of boxing represents the ultimate test of skill, will, and sacrifice. Called the "noble art," it has been praised by such world leaders as Theodore Roosevelt and Winston Churchill. But boxing also has a dark side. The sport that famed sportswriter Jimmy Cannon called the "red light district of sports" has been beset with numerous ring deaths.

Here are some of the more high-profile ring deaths that have had a devastating effect upon the sport of boxing.

1. EMILE GRIFFITH TKO 12 BENNY "KID" PARET

Hall of Famer Emile Griffith, one of the greatest welterweights of all time, faced his nemesis, Benny "Kid" Paret, for the third time in Madison Square Garden. The pair had a short and heated history. In April 1961, Griffith captured his first world title by coming from behind and stopping Paret in the thirteenth round in Miami Beach. However, in September 1961, the two faced off again in New York. Paret recaptured his crown via a disputed fifteen-round split decision.

That set the stage for the rubber match between the two talented foes in March 1962—again in Madison Square Garden. Griffith battered Paret senseless in the twelfth round until referee Ruby Goldstein finally stopped the bout. The scene of Paret lying helpless on the ropes taking punches will never leave anyone who sees footage of the bout. Paret died during surgery to relieve pressure on his brain. Many believed that Goldstein reacted too slowly in stopping the bout. He never refereed another bout. Paret's death affected Griffith, too. "I would have quit," he said, "but I didn't know how to do anything else." Griffith continued to fight, adding the middleweight title to his resume.

Historian Jeffrey Sammons writes in his book *Beyond the Ring*: "The [Paret] tragedy evoked a worldwide outpouring of criticism and denunciation of boxing, along with a host of meaningless investigations that centered on whether referee Ruby Goldstein had acted properly; whether doctors had failed to detect prior injuries; or whether ruthless managers had pushed their warrior into a fight before he had fully recovered from recent beatings."

2. RAY MANCINI TKO 14 DUK KOO KIM

The popular Ray "Boom Boom" Mancini knew only one way to fight—as a whirling dervish. He had a crowd-pleasing, brawling style that endeared him to the boxing public. On November 13, 1982, in the second defense of his crown, he met an unheralded Korean named Duk Koo Kim in Las Vegas, Nevada. The son of a rice farmer, Kim had scribbled "Kill or Be Killed" on his hotel wall before the fight. His writing would prove prophetic.

Mancini and Kim waged war, with Kim actually winning a few rounds. But gradually Mancini began to take control, inflicting a beating on the courageous Korean. Still, Kim continued to throw punches. He never backed down and continued to be more game than perhaps he should have been. Mancini kayoed Kim in the fourteenth round. The unconscious Kim had to be taken from the ring on a stretcher. He never awoke and died four days later on November 17, 1982.

This bout caused reverberations felt round the boxing world. In December 1982, the World Boxing Council officially changed the length of its championship bouts from fifteen rounds to twelve rounds as a direct result of the fight. Tragically, two others connected to the bout killed themselves within a year—Kim's mother and Richard Greene, who refereed the bout.

3. RAY ROBINSON KO 8 JIMMY DOYLE

In June 1947, Sugar Ray Robinson, the world welterweight champion, defended his title against an overmatched Jimmy Doyle in Cleveland, Ohio. Robinson apparently had premonitions before the fight that he would hurt Doyle in the bout. He dreamt that his opponent would die in the ring. Robinson said he did not want to fight, but the promoters of the event brought in a Catholic priest who convinced Robinson to fight, and his conscience was clear.

Robinson's dream became a nightmarish reality as he battered the overmatched Doyle until the referee stopped the bout in the eighth round. When asked at the coroner's inquest if he knew that he had Doyle in trouble, Robinson answered: "They pay me to get them in trouble." But Doyle's death took its toll even on the great Sugar Ray Robinson. In his autobiography, *Sugar*

Ray, he relates: "For weeks, I had trouble sleeping. Whenever my mind wasn't occupied, I'd see Doyle's blank eyes staring up at me from the canvas."

4. ULTIMINIO "SUGAR" RAMOS TKO 10 DAVEY MOORE

Davey Moore, the "Springfield Rifle," was the popular world featherweight champion from 1959 to 1963. In his final fight, he defended his title against Ultiminio "Sugar" Ramos, a future boxing Hall of Famer from Cuba. The two met in March 1963 in Los Angeles, California. Ramos was physically stronger and eight years younger than Moore. The two fighters fought fiercely. In the tenth round, Ramos hit the champion with a series of punches that knocked Moore into the ropes. His head snapped back after hitting the bottom rope.

Moore exited the ring, beaten but seemingly fine. He walked to his dressing room and addressed reporters. "Sure, I want to fight him [Ramos] again. And I'll get the title back." Instead, he died four days later on March 25. Doctors attributed his death to damage caused by his head striking the bottom rope.

The fight caused television networks to shun boxing for a short time. The fight also inspired legendary performer Bob Dylan to write the song, "Who Killed Davey Moore?" The popular song begins with the refrain: "Who killed Davey Moore / Why an' what's the reason for?" The powerful song contains verses in which the referee, the crowd, the manager, the gambling man, the boxing writer, and Moore's opponent all claim it was not their fault. Ironically, Moore was the second opponent to die after a fight with Sugar Ramos.

5. GEORGE KHALID JONES TKO 10 BEETHAEVEN SCOTTLAND

Up-and-coming light heavyweight George Khalid Jones was undefeated heading into his June 2001 clash with contender and former world challenger David Telesco. Jones had resumed his career after a short prison stint and had turned his life around in a positive direction. Unfortunately, Telesco pulled out of the fight and was replaced on short notice by the lesser-known Beethaeven "Bee" Scottland, who usually fought as a super middleweight.

Jones dominated the early and middle rounds, battering Scottland to the extent that ESPN2 boxing analyst Max Kellerman cried out for the fight to be stopped. But somehow Scottland managed to survive and actually win the eighth and ninth rounds on two of the official scorecards. But with only thirty-seven seconds left in the tenth round, Jones tagged Scottland with a left hook followed by a right hand that dropped Scottland. He slipped into a coma. Emergency surgery could not revive the game warrior, and he died six days later. The fight placed the New York State Athletic Commission under a microscope and questions remain whether referee Arthur Mercante Jr. should have stopped the fight sooner.

Jones continues to pursue his boxing career. In his next fight, he took a giant step up in class and lost to top contender Eric Harding. The tragedy still affects Jones. When asked about it in an exclusive Fightnews .com interview with David Hudson, coauthor of this book, Jones said:

It affected me deeply. For the first six weeks, I had a lot of depression. I was in down spirits and basically kept to myself. But with the help of friends, spiritual advisors, and professional help, I came to grips with it. It did happen in a sporting event, not a street brawl.

It helped me a lot to go to Bee Scottland's funeral. I mean it was real tough to go there, but his family showed no anger to me and said that I showed class by coming to the funeral. Several members of his family came up and shook my hand and told me, "Now go on and win a world title, so we can say that Bee lost to the best."

6. LUPE PINTOR KO 12 JOHNNY OWEN

In September 1980, Mexico's Lupe Pintor defended his world bantamweight crown against a young Welsh opponent named Johnny Owen, called the "Merthyr Matchstick Man." Owen was the European bantamweight champion, but when he went to Los Angeles to face the stronger Pintor, he was overmatched. Pintor pressed the action against the game Owen and floored him in the ninth round and twice in the twelfth round. Owen died forty-five days later. In May 2002, a statue of Johnny Owen was erected in his hometown. An honored guest at the unveiling was none other than Lupe Pintor.

7. WILFORD SCYPION KO 10 WILLIE CLASSEN

In November 1979, middleweight prospect Wilford Scypion was 12–0 with twelve knockouts. A strong puncher, Scypion was being groomed for a championship. He soon would step up and face tougher competition. But first he faced Willie Classen of the Bronx, who sported a mediocre record of 16–7–2. Scypion battered Classen throughout much of the bout in New York City, dropping him several times. Scypion finished off the game Classen in the tenth and final round.

Classen died of a brain hemorrhage five days after the bout. His widow sued Madison Square Garden, two ringside physicians, and the referee for failing to provide adequate medical care and failing to promptly take Classen to the hospital. Documents showed that it took thirty minutes for an ambulance to arrive to take the fallen fighter to the hospital. In 1987, Marilyn Classen received what was reported to be a six-figure settlement from attorneys for the two doctors and Madison Square Garden. The fight had major ramifications on boxing in New York.

The New York Times reported in a November 1987 article:

> Mr. Classen's death, of a brain hemorrhage five days later, resulted in various reforms in boxing safety rules and state-mandated medical procedures in the early 1980's. For example, New York State now requires that an ambulance be posted at all boxing matches, and professional boxing officials have adopted what is called the Classen Rule, which says a fighter must make it to the center of the ring under his own power at the start of each round.

Scypion went on to have a productive career, though he was overwhelmed in four rounds by Marvelous Marvin Hagler in his only world title shot in 1983.

8. DAVID GONZALEZ TKO 9 ROBERT WANGILA

The story of Robert Wangila has all the elements of a poignant Hollywood screenplay. At the 1988 Seoul Olympics, Wangila of Kenya became the first boxer from Africa to capture an Olympic gold medal. He was a national hero. Then he turned pro. As *Los Angeles Times* boxing scribe Tim Kawakami wrote in a July 1994 article: "Robert Wangila spent six years futilely attempting to relive his one, golden flash." He never could—and he died trying.

In 1994, Wangila entered the ring in Las Vegas against top-ten contender David Gonzales of Houston, Texas. Wangila possessed above-average offensive skills but was not as proficient on the defensive side. He relied on his ability to absorb punishment. Wangila started strongly but faded as the fight progressed. By the eighth round, Gonzales had taken control. The referee stopped the bout in the ninth round. Wangila appeared to be fine, other than being upset at his fifth loss. Then he died of brain injuries caused by the pounding he took in the ring. Ironically, Wangila was not the first professional opponent of Gonzalez to die of ring-related injuries. Rico Velasquez, Gonzalez's second opponent, died in an El Paso hospital after Gonzalez kayoed him for the Texas lightweight title. Gonzales failed in his only world title bout when Terry Norris stopped him for the world junior middleweight championship.

9. GABRIEL RUELAS TKO 11 JIMMY GARCIA

The popular Gabriel Ruelas made the second defense of his WBC super featherweight title against challenger Jimmy Garcia in May 1995 in Las Vegas, Nevada. Overwhelmed by the power punching of Ruelas, Garcia bravely struggled into the later rounds. But he was too brave for his own good. Garcia died thirteen days after the bout.

Ruelas was never the same fighter after the Garcia bout. In his next fight, a rematch with the great Azumah

Nelson, he gave a listless performance. Those close to him said the Garcia fight haunted him. Ruelas retired for a time but has resumed his career. He hopes to land a title fight in the lightweight division by the end of 2002 or in 2003. He says: "Without a doubt, the Jimmy Garcia fight was and will always be the low point of my career."

10.　GAETAN HART KO 10 CLEVELAND DENNY

In 1978, Gaetan Hart won a ten-round decision over Cleveland Denny for the Canadian lightweight title. Two years later, the two rivals fought a rematch on the undercard of the first fight between all-time greats Sugar Ray Leonard and Roberto Duran—the so-called Brawl in Montreal held in June 1980. Though Leonard–Duran I may be more remembered, it was the second bout of the evening that had the greatest tragedy. In that bout, Hart kayoed Denny with only twelve seconds left in the final round. The fight was close, as Denny had won the eighth and ninth rounds. Alan Goldstein recalls the bout in his book on Sugar Ray Leonard entitled *A Fistful of Sugar*: "Instant replay showed Denny, slumped against the rope, absorbing a dozen savage blows to the head before referee Rosario Baillargeon stood behind Hart waving his arms to signal the fight was over—arms Hart couldn't see as he continued to pummel Denny."

Denny died seventeen days later after falling into a coma. In his previous bout, Hart had put his opponent, Ralph Racine, into a coma for four days and ended his career. Hart continued his career, losing in the fourth round to Aaron Pryor in a world junior welterweight title bout. He even fought in 2000 after another ill-fated comeback at the age of forty-seven.

Death Behind the Wheel

The sport of boxing has been beset by countless tragedies both in and out of the ring. Every year thousands of people die in automobile accidents. Boxers are not immune to this alarming fact of life. Indeed, many boxers have died as a result of automobile accidents. Here is a list of ten boxers who suffered this fate.

1. JACK JOHNSON

Jack Johnson, the world's first African-American heavyweight champion, defied society's conventions in many ways, from dalliances with and marriages to white women to taunting overmatched opponents. Johnson also loved fast and flashy automobiles. Legend has it that once while Johnson was driving through Georgia, a police officer stopped him for speeding, which carried a twenty-five-dollar fine. Johnson handed the officer fifty dollars and told the cop to keep the change. When the stunned officer asked why, Johnson replied: "I've got to come back through this road on the way back." He died in an automobile crash near Raleigh, North Carolina, while traveling to the second Joe Louis–Billy Conn fight in 1946.

2. SALVADOR SANCHEZ

The great Salvador Sanchez dominated the featherweight division with splendid boxing skills during the late 1970s and early 1980s. Unfortunately, we will never know how much Sanchez could have added to his Hall of Fame career because he wrecked his red Porsche in the early morning hours of August 12, 1982. He was in the midst of training for an upcoming title defense against Juan LaPorte.

3. CARLOS MONZON

Argentina's legendary Carlos Monzon ruled the middleweight division from 1970 to 1975, making a then-record fourteen title defenses. He retired with an incredible record of 87–3–9. But life outside the ring did not go as well for this champion. In 1988, he was convicted of killing his estranged lover, Alicia Muniz, by throwing her off a balcony. In 1995, Monzon was driving back to prison after spending the day on a furlough. He never made it back, as his car ran off the road and he died.

4. VICTOR GALINDEZ

Victor Galindez of Argentina twice won the world light heavyweight championship, in 1974 and 1979. A rough-and-tough slugger, Galindez also picked up considerable boxing skills as his career advanced, including tips from his friend and countryman Carlos Monzon. Galindez retired in June 1980 and, tragically, lived only four more months. Upon retirement, Galindez turned his energies to auto racing. In October 1980, he rode with racer Antonio Lizeviche in competition. When their car stalled, they exited the race car on the track and were struck by another racing car.

5. JOE WALCOTT

Joe Walcott, "The Barbados Demon," stood less than 5'2" but was a giant in the ring. The world welterweight champion from 1901 to 1904, Walcott also regularly fought and beat men who outweighed him by thirty to fifty pounds. For example, in 1900 he even knocked out heavyweight Joe Choynski, a Hall of Fame fighter. He died in 1935 in Massillon, Ohio, when a car struck him.

6. YOUNG STRIBLING

Young Stribling, called the "King of the Canebrakes," was a top light heavyweight and heavyweight in the 1920s and early 1930s. Though he lost in world title bids in both divisions, he recorded 221 wins and 125 knockouts in his illustrious career. In September 1933, Stribling won a ten-round decision over fellow Hall of Famer Maxie Rosenbloom. He never fought again, because the next month a car struck and killed him while he was riding his motorcycle.

7. MASAO OHBA

Japan's Masao Ohba captured the WBA world flyweight title in 1970 in Tokyo. Possessing a great left jab, he successfully defended his title five times. Ohba was a national hero in his native land, where he fought all but one of his bouts. Tragically, he lost his life a mere twenty-two days after his last defense. He was killed in a car crash outside Tokyo at the age of twenty-three.

8. DAVEY MOORE

Davey Moore won the World Boxing Association's junior middleweight championship in only his ninth pro bout. He successfully defended his crown three times before losing to the legendary Roberto "Hands of Stone" Duran in 1983. Moore began a comeback in 1988, winning two fights. He planned to fight for another world title, but it was not to be. In June, he parked his Jeep on a steep slope and began to carry grocery bags into his home. When the Jeep began to slide down the hill, Moore tried to stop it, slipped, and was run over. He died instantly at the age of twenty-nine.

9. BILLY COLLINS JR.

In June 1983, undefeated welterweight Billy Collins Jr. was sitting on the cusp of stardom. Fighting on the undercard of the Davey Moore–Roberto Duran title fight in New York, he faced Luis Resto. Surprisingly, Resto pounded Collins over ten rounds. Collins's father felt Resto's gloves after the fight and realized why his son was beaten so badly. Someone had taken most of the stuffing out of Resto's gloves. Resto and his trainer, Panama Lewis, later served jail time for the incident. But Collins Jr. fared even worse. The beating he took in the fight ended his career. Then, nine months later, despondent over the end of his boxing career, he died in a car accident while drinking. He was only twenty-two years old.

10. NOBUTOSHI HIRANAKA

Japan's Nobutoshi Hiranaka was a world-rated featherweight contender who twice fought for a world title unsuccessfully in 1995 and 1996. Hiranaka, the younger brother of one-time WBA super lightweight champion Akinobu Hiranaka, then moved up to the super feather-weight division. In March 2000, he was killed when his car crashed into a utility pole outside Okinawa. He was only thirty-one years of age.

"Suicide Solution"

The sport of boxing has always had more than its share of hard-luck stories and tragic endings. Perhaps that's why well-known writer Joyce Carol Oates referred to boxing as "the cruelest sport" in her elegantly written book, *On Boxing*. Unfortunately, many boxers have taken their own lives, whether by gun, rope, automobile, or by jumping off a building. Some took their lives while their careers were still active. Others took their lives after they retired, long after the public adulation and money had run out.

The following is a list of boxers and/or referees who took their own lives.

1. BILLY PAPKE

Billy Papke, known as the "Illinois Thunderbolt," went through life in a violent fashion from beginning to end. He turned pro as a middleweight in 1906 and two years later won the world title by stopping the great Stanley Ketchel in a bloody battle. Papke stunned Ketchel in the opening round by smacking the champion to the ground with a right hand as Ketchel had his hands extended in greeting. Ketchel defeated him in a rematch.

He lost another attempt at the world title in March 1913. He retired in 1919 but ultimately could never escape his violent past. On Thanksgiving Day in 1936, Papke shot his estranged wife and then killed himself.

2. CHARLES "KID" MCCOY

Charles "Kid" McCoy was one of the most unusual characters to ever enter a boxing ring. He was called the "Corkscrew Kid" because he invented the damaging "corkscrew punch," which was given with a twist at the point of contact to cause more damage. McCoy won the world middleweight title in 1897 and then moved up to the heavyweight division. McCoy retired in 1916 and never found stability outside the ring. He was convicted of manslaughter for killing his lover and served twenty-four years in prison. He killed himself in 1940.

3. AARON LISTER BROWN (THE DIXIE KID)

Only the most knowledgeable of boxing historians would know the name Aaron Lister Brown, the given name of "The Dixie Kid," an early African-American fighter who won the world welterweight championship in 1904 by defeating the great Joe Walcott. The Dixie Kid fought with a unique style, holding his hands by his side and daring opponents to strike him. He retired in 1920 with more than 150 pro bouts. In April 1934, The Kid fell off a tenement window to his death in Los Angeles, California. Some speculate the "fall" was not accidental.

4. RANDY TURPIN

Randy Turpin was a world middleweight champion who upset the great Sugar Ray Robinson in July 1951. Turpin was known as the "Leamington Licker" because he was born in Leamington, England, and could lick any fighter placed in front of him. Turpin lost his world title to Robinson in a rematch in 1951 and never won another world title. He lost a fifteen-round decision to Carl "Bobo" Olson in 1953 in his only other championship bout. Beset by personal problems and tax difficulties, Turpin killed his seventeen-month-old daughter, Carmen, and then shot himself in 1966.

5.   FREDDIE MILLS

"Fearless" Freddie Mills was a world light heavyweight champion known for his tremendous courage in the ring. He won the world title in July 1948 with a fifteen-round decision over Gus Lesnevich. He lost his world title in his last bout, suffering a brutal beating from Hall of Famer Joey Maxim over ten rounds. Throughout his career, Englishman Mills faced many heavyweights who outweighed him by twenty or thirty pounds. Mills retired after the Maxim loss, suffering continuing headaches. In 1965, Mills was found dead inside his car with a rifle wound to his head. A coroner determined that the cause of death was suicide.

6.   RICKEY WOMACK

Rickey Womack was a world-class amateur boxer who defeated Evander Holyfield three times in the light heavyweight division while both were amateurs. However, Holyfield bested him twice in a row to win a spot on the 1984 Olympic team. Womack turned pro and earned a draw in his debut. He then won ten straight bouts from 1984 to 1985. Many believed he couldn't miss becoming world champion. However, Womack was convicted of armed robbery and served fourteen years in prison. Released in November 2000, he returned to boxing as a cruiserweight. He won four straight bouts. Then, in January 2002, he shot and killed himself. He was forty.

7. SEIJI TAKECHI

Seiji Takechi was the two-time Orient and Pacific junior middleweight champion and a world-rated boxer by the World Boxing Council (WBC) in May 2001. He had compiled a record of 10–3–2 draws and was never knocked out. Unfortunately, Takechi never fought for a world title because he took his own life in August 2001. The twenty-four-year-old was found hanging from a rope tied to a fence outside a shrine. Police presumed that he killed himself.

8. GABRIEL HERNANDEZ

Gabriel Hernandez fought for his home country, the Dominican Republic, in the 1996 Olympic Games in Atlanta. He also won a bronze medal at the 1995 Pan American Games. He turned pro after the Olympics and quickly compiled a record of 13–0–2. In May 1999, he received a shot at the IBF super middleweight world championship. He lost a unanimous twelve-round decision to champion Sven Ottke. He continued fighting, losing only one more bout. In June 2002, he won in the first round against a nondescript opponent. About a week later, he hung himself. He left behind a wife and three kids. He was only twenty-seven.

9. MITCH HALPERN

Mitch Halpern was one of boxing's best referees at the time of his tragic suicide at the age of thirty-three in 2000. He had worked numerous world title bouts in his hometown of Las Vegas, Nevada, including the historic first fight between Evander Holyfield and Mike Tyson. Speculation abounded as to why this young man, at the top of his profession, tragically took his own life. Possible explanations included a recent fight with his fiancée, his mother's diagnosis of breast cancer, and the death of Jimmy Garcia in a bout with Gabriel Ruelas refereed by Halpern. Whatever the reason, boxing lost one of its brightest stars when Halpern took his own life.

10.   RICHARD GREENE

By the early 1980s, Richard Greene was one of the most active and best referees in the world. Based in the fight mecca of Las Vegas, Greene worked numerous world title bouts. In November 1982, he was the third man in the ring in a classic battle between champion Ray "Boom Boom" Mancini and courageous challenger Duk Koo Kim. Greene stopped the bout in the fourteenth round, but Kim never recovered from the beating. Not too long after Kim's death, Greene shot himself in the head. Some speculated that he could not forgive himself for the Kim tragedy.

Like Father, Like Son

M any sons grow up following in the footsteps of their fathers. Boxing is no exception, as many fighters have watched their sons also pursue boxing careers. Many times the son's ring accomplishments do not match the father's. For example, Marvis Frazier, a good heavyweight in his own right, simply could not match his legendary father, "Smokin" Joe Frazier. Other times, the son achieves far more in the ring than his father ever did. The story of Ray Mancini adopting his father's nickname of "Boom Boom" and winning a world title for his father, who never got a title shot, is particularly heartwarming.

1. JOE AND MARVIS FRAZIER

"Smokin" Joe Frazier was a warrior from Philadelphia who captured Olympic gold in 1964 and later the world heavyweight championship. He is best known for his classic trilogy with his rival, Muhammad Ali. His son, Marvis Frazier, fought as a heavyweight for most of the 1980s. A small heavyweight without his father's fearsome left hook, Marvis could not reach the same level as his father, though he did receive a world heavyweight title shot in 1983 against Larry Holmes. Holmes stopped the younger Frazier in the first round. Frazier later lost to Mike Tyson in a thirty-second stoppage. He finished with a record of 19–2.

2. FLOYD (SR.) AND FLOYD (JR.) MAYWEATHER

Floyd Mayweather Sr. was a talented welterweight from Michigan who never reached the peak of his profession as a boxer, unlike his brother, Roger Mayweather, and son, Floyd Jr. He lost to future world champions Sugar Ray Leonard and Marlon "Magic Man" Starling. His career ended due to a drug conviction for which he served ten years in prison. Mayweather is considered one of the sport's top trainers. His son, "Pretty Boy" Floyd Mayweather Jr., is one of the best pound-for-pound boxers in the world today. Still unbeaten, he has captured world titles in the super featherweight and lightweight divisions.

3. BILL AND "BUSTER" DOUGLAS

Bill (Billy) "Dynamite" Douglas was a tough middleweight and light heavyweight contender who fought from 1967 to 1980. He never received a world title shot, but he fought the likes of Bennie Briscoe, Willie Monroe, Victor Galindez, Matthew Saad Muhammad, and Marvin Johnson. Bill's son, James "Buster" Douglas, fought as a heavyweight. A career underachiever who did not seem to possess the same fire in the belly as his father, Buster nevertheless achieved boxing immortality with his stunning 1990 upset of world champion and supposedly invincible "Iron" Mike Tyson. Douglas reverted to form and lost the title in his very first defense against Evander Holyfield.

4. **GUTY (SR.) AND GUTY (JR.) ESPADAS**

Guty Espadas captured the WBA flyweight championship in 1976 with a late-round stoppage of then-
unbeaten Alfonzo Lopez. He defended his title four
times, winning all by knockout. He lost his title on
points in 1978 and never won another world title. He
retired in 1984 after losing in a bid for the WBC world
flyweight title. His son, Guty Espadas Jr., won the WBC
featherweight championship in 2000, making the
Espadas the first father–son combination to both capture world titles. Espadas lost his title in his second defense in a very controversial decision loss to Erik
Morales. At the time of this writing, he remains a top
contender in the featherweight division.

5. **JOE AND CHRIS BYRD**

Joe Byrd fought as a heavyweight in the 1960s and
1970s. He lost more fights than he won, including a
kayo loss to fearsome puncher Earnie Shavers. He retired in 1972 after losing his fourth fight in a row. Joe
has had more success as the trainer/manager of his
son, Chris Byrd. An Olympic silver medalist at 168
pounds in 1992, Chris Byrd put on weight and campaigned as a heavyweight. His boxing skills and defensive abilities have enabled him to beat many top
heavyweights, including power-puncher David Tua. In
December 2002, Chris Byrd outboxed Evander Holyfield to win the IBF world heavyweight championship.

6. **LENNY AND RAY MANCINI**

Lenny "Boom Boom" Mancini was a tough-as-nails, in-
your-face lightweight from Youngstown, Ohio, who
fought professionally in the late 1930s and 1940s. He

Chris Cozzone

Chris Byrd rocks power puncher David Tua. Under the
tutelage of his father/trainer/manager Joe, Byrd went on to
win the IBF world heavyweight championship from Evander
Holyfield in December 2002.

was stopped only once in his career but never received
a world title shot. His son, Ray Mancini, adopted his
father's nickname and became an instant American
hero. In 1983, the popular Mancini captured the world
title his father never had an opportunity to win with a
first-round kayo of Art Frias for the WBA title. He defended his title four times until a decision loss to the
tough Livingstone Bramble.

7. FLOYD AND TRACY HARRIS PATTERSON

Floyd Patterson was the first two-time world heavyweight champion and a former Olympic gold medalist.
Considered a good guy, Patterson received a national
award from President John F. Kennedy for being a pos-

itive role model. He lost his title to Sonny Liston in the first round in 1962. He retired after a second loss to Muhammad Ali in 1972. Patterson took a keen interest in a young kid named Tracy Harris who was learning how to box. Patterson eventually adopted the youngster. In 1992, Tracy Harris Patterson followed in his father's footsteps by winning a world title. He stopped Thierry Jacob in the second round to win the WBC super bantamweight title. In 1995, he added a second title with a second-round stoppage of unbeaten Ed Hopson for the IBF super featherweight title.

8.   HECTOR (SR.) AND HECTOR (JR.) CAMACHO

Hector Camacho Sr. and Jr. fought on the same card in Miami, Florida, in March 2001, both posting wins. The elder Camacho, who calls himself "Macho" Camacho, was a blazing talent with incredible speed in his prime. He won major world titles at super featherweight and lightweight. He defeated fighters such as Bazooka Limon, Jose Luis Ramirez, and Edwin Rosario. He posted wins over Sugar Ray Leonard in 1997 and Roberto Duran in 2001, when those legends were even further past their primes than Camacho. Camacho Jr. is a welterweight contender who at the time of this writing has lost only once in more than thirty bouts.

9.   TOM AND PETER MCNEELEY

Tom and Peter McNeeley were heavyweights who lost the biggest fights of their careers. Tom fought from 1958 to 1966, compiling a record of 31–14. He lost in the fourth round to Floyd Patterson in his only world title shot in 1961. Peter "Hurricane" McNeeley racked up more than forty wins against inferior opposition. He will forever be known as Mike Tyson's first opponent after the ex-champion's three-year prison sentence for rape. McNeeley didn't make it out of the first round. He later lost to Eric "Butterbean" Esch in the first round as well.

10. LEON AND CORY SPINKS

Leon "Neon" Spinks won an Olympic gold medal in the 1976 Olympics and then upset Muhammad Ali in 1978 to win the world heavyweight title in only his ninth pro bout. Unfortunately, his career took a nosedive after he lost a rematch to Ali. Cory "Next Generation" Spinks is a talented junior welterweight champion with a record of 31–2. His only losses were by controversial decisions, including a twelve-round loss to Italian Michele Piccirillo in Italy for the IBF world title. Cory avenged the loss to Piccirillo in March 2003 to win the IBF title by unanimous decision.

Boxing Brothers

Sports stars often come from the same bloodlines. Boxing is no exception. Brothers Joe (welterweight) and Vince Dundee (middleweight) won world titles in the 1920s and 1930s, respectively. Currently, the towering Ukrainian stars Wladimir and Vitali Klitschko are both top-ten rated heavyweights intent on dominating the division and securing the sport's crown jewel. However, the two brothers say they will never fight each other. There have been many boxing brothers. Some of the boxing brothers include a rather famous fighter and a lesser-known sibling. Muhammad Ali's brother, Rudy, for instance, boxed some as a professional though he never became a contender. The brothers in this list all were champions or contenders in their respective weight divisions.

1. LEON AND MICHAEL SPINKS

The Spinks brothers first vaulted into national prominence at the 1976 Montreal Olympic Games by capturing gold medals. Leon won at light heavyweight and Michael at middleweight. In the professional ranks, Leon struck gold first in 1978, winning the world title in only his ninth pro fight in a shocking upset of the great Muhammad Ali. He lost in a rematch seven months later. He later lost a 1981 title bid against Larry Holmes. While Leon won his world title first, Michael unquestionably had the better career. In July 1981, Michael won the WBA light heavyweight belt from Eddie Mustafa Muhammad. He consolidated the belts with a win over the tough Dwight Braxton in 1983. After cleaning out his division, Spinks did the unthinkable—defeating the 48–0 Larry Holmes to capture the IBF world heavyweight crown. His only defeat in thirty-two pro bouts was a 1988 loss to Mike Tyson.

2. MIKE AND TOMMY GIBBONS

St. Paul, Minnesota, produced the only pair of brothers elected to the International Boxing Hall of Fame—Mike and Tommy Gibbons. Mike fought as a middleweight from 1908 until 1922. Opponents had a hard time hitting the lighter Gibbons brother, who was known as the "St. Paul Phantom." He lost only three times in 127 total bouts. Tommy Gibbons began as a welterweight in 1911 but ended up as a heavyweight in a career that lasted until 1925. He lost a fifteen-round decision to Jack Dempsey for the world title. He retired after being stopped for the only time in his career by future world heavyweight champion Gene Tunney. Tommy later served multiple terms as the sheriff of St. Paul.

3. GABRIEL AND RAFAEL RUELAS

Gabriel and Rafael Ruelas have the distinction of being the second pair of brothers to simultaneously hold world titles. Born in Jalisco, Mexico, the Ruelas brothers moved to California in their formative years. Legend has it that they appeared on the doorstep of prominent trainer Joe Goosen, who took the boys under his wing. Goosen must have seen something in the boys at that early age, because in 1994 both brothers captured world titles. Rafael, the younger brother, won the IBF lightweight crown with a twelve-round decision over the dangerous Freddie Pendleton. He defended the title twice before a devastating loss to Oscar De La Hoya in May 1995. Gabriel won the WBC super featherweight crown in September 1994 with a decision win over the previously undefeated Jesse James Leija. Gabriel also defended his title twice before losing to the great Azumah Nelson in December 1995.

4. KHAOSAI AND KHAOKOR GALAXY

Khaosai and Khaokor Galaxy are the first pair of twins to become world boxing champions. The Galaxy brothers began their careers as kickboxers in the sport known as Thai boxing. But they achieved worldwide fame in traditional boxing. Khaosai, known as the "Thai Tyson," dominated the junior bantamweight division from 1984 until his retirement in 1991. He made nineteen defenses of his crown, sixteen by knockout. His record was an amazing 50–1 with forty-four kayoes. He was inducted into the International Boxing Hall of Fame in 1999. Khaokor Galaxy won the WBA bantamweight title in 1988 with a twelve-round decision over Wilfredo Vasquez. He lost his title via a technical decision in his first defense against Sung-Kil Moon. In 1989, Khaokor regained his title from Moon. He retired after losing badly in his next bout.

5. CHANA AND SONGKRAM PORPAOIN

The Porpaoin brothers became the second pair of twin brothers to win world titles. The Thai brothers won belts

in boxing's lightest weight class—the minimumweight
or strawweight division. Chana won the WBA minimumweight title in February 1993 and made eight successful defenses before losing a twelve-round split
decision to Rosendo Alvarez in December 1995. He recaptured the belt in April 2001 and then lost it in his
first defense. He continues to box. Songkram won the
WBA minimumweight belt in January 1999 with a
technical decision win over Ronnie Magramo. He never
made a title defense because he was stripped of the
title. He also continues to fight.

6. MAX AND BUDDY BAER

Maximillian Adalbert Baer and Jacob Henry Baer are
better known by their nicknames, Max and Buddy. Max
was the better fighter and the one who won a world title.
In June 1934, Baer defeated the giant Primo Carnera,
dropping him eleven times in eleven rounds. Possessed
with great talent and tremendous power in his right
hand, Baer was also a notorious playboy who did not
train with great zeal. He lost in his first title defense to
James Braddock. At 6'6½", Buddy Baer stood four
inches taller than his older brother, but he could not
reach as high in boxing as Max did. Buddy's problem
was Joe Louis, who twice defeated him, in May 1941
and January 1942, in world title bouts. In the second
bout, Louis blasted him out in the first round.

7. TONY AND MIKE AYALA

Tony and Mike Ayala might have both been world
champions under different circumstances. Trained by
their father, Tony Sr., a tough disciplinarian, the brothers from San Antonio, Texas, never quite made it to the
top of their respective divisions. Mike Ayala possessed

great boxing skills but wasted his skills and reportedly fell victim to drug abuse. He did fight well enough to earn three title shots in his career. He lost all three bouts, including a 1979 classic for the featherweight title against Danny "Little Red" Lopez. Tony "El Torrito" Ayala is an even sadder case. In the early 1980s, every boxing expert picked this terror to win the junior middleweight belt. Unfortunately, he was convicted of rape and served sixteen years in jail. He returned to the ring upon his release in 1999 and has encountered additional legal problems.

8. DONALD AND BRUCE CURRY

Donald and Bruce Curry became the first pair of brothers to hold world titles at the same time. They both captured world titles in the 1980s, though Donald was clearly the better fighter. With fast hands, flashy feet, and power, Donald "The Lone Star Cobra" Curry dominated the welterweight division in the 1980s, unifying the title by capturing all three major belts. His best performance was his spectacular kayo over fellow champion Milton McCrory in 1985. He added the WBC light middleweight belt to his resume in 1987 but lost it in his first defense. His skills in decline, he lost to Michael Nunn and Terry Norris in back-to-back title shots in the early 1990s. Bruce Curry, known for his powerful left hook, was a perennial contender until a 1983 victory over Leroy Haley earned him the WBC light welterweight title. He defended the title twice.

9. MILTON AND STEVE MCCRORY

Milton "Ice Man" McCrory and his younger brother, Steve, were top fighters in legendary trainer Emmanuel Steward's Kronk gym in Detroit, Michigan. Milton captured the WBC welterweight title in August 1983. He made four defenses of his crown to run his record to an impressive 26–0–1, until he faced fellow unbeaten welterweight champ Donald Curry for the undisputed championship. In the biggest fight of his career, McCrory lost in the second round. He never again won a world title, losing in a bid for the WBA light middleweight crown in 1987. He retired for good ten years later. Steve McCrory won the Olympic flyweight gold medal at the 1984 Los Angeles Olympics. He lost in his only world title bid to future Hall of Famer Jeff Fenech in 1986. He died in 2000 of a prolonged illness.

10. **JERRY AND MIKE QUARRY**

Jerry and Mike Quarry were a pair of popular California fighters in the heavyweight and light heavyweight divisions, respectively, who never quite made it to the top. Jerry Quarry was a boxer-puncher who fought many top heavyweights, including world champions Muhammad Ali, Joe Frazier, Jimmy Ellis, and Ken Norton. Though he lost to them all, Quarry had wins over such fighters as Floyd Patterson, Ron Lyle, and Earnie Shavers. Mike Quarry was a longtime contender in the light heavyweight division. In 1972, he lost to world champion Bob Foster in the fourth round in his only title shot. He compiled more than sixty wins in a lengthy pro career that spanned from 1969 to 1982. A third Quarry brother, Bobby, also fought professionally, though he had a losing record.

She Can Fight, Too

In the 1970s, the sport of boxing was dominated by great heavyweights Muhammad Ali, "Smokin" Joe Frazier, and George Foreman. Fast-forward to 2000 and the sport still has an Ali, a Frazier, and a Foreman battling for ring supremacy. But it's the daughters who are running the show now, as Laila Ali, Jacqui Frazier-Lyde, and Freeda Foreman have all followed in their famous fathers' footsteps. There are other female fighters who have famous male-relative boxers. The following is a list of ten such fighters.

1. LAILA ALI

Laili Ali is the fastest-rising woman's boxing star and the daughter of the great Muhammad Ali. In the eyes of many, she is considered the future of women's boxing. She also has crossover star appeal, appearing on the cover of various magazines and playing roles in different sitcom episodes. As of October 2003, Laila had an undefeated record of 16–0 with ten kayoes. She holds an eight-round majority decision victory over Jacqui Frazier-Lyde, the daughter of "Smokin" Joe Frazier.

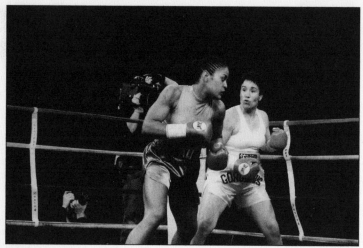

Scott Romer

The undefeated daughter of legendary Muhammad Ali,
Laila Ali (left) fights against Mary Ann Almager.

2. JACQUI FRAZIER-LYDE

The daughter of "Smokin" Joe Frazier, Frazier-Lyde
has gone from being a successful college basketball
player to an attorney to a professional boxer. As of October 2003, Frazier-Lyde had compiled a record of
11–1 with nine kayoes. Her only loss was a tough decision loss to the younger Laila Ali.

3. FREEDA FOREMAN

Much to the dismay of her famous father, George Foreman, Freeda Foreman has followed in the footsteps of
Laila Ali and Jacqui Frazier-Lyde. She turned pro in
2000 and has a record of 5–1. Her father does not want
her to keep fighting and reportedly offered her money
to stop fighting after her first bout.

4. **IRICHELLE DURAN**

Irichelle Duran is a bantamweight and the daughter of legendary Roberto "Hands of Stone" Duran. The great Duran reportedly would not speak to his daughter for a week after learning of her intentions to box professionally. She has a record of 2–2.

5. **MARIA JOHANSSON**

Maria Johansson is the daughter of former world heavyweight champion Ingemar Johansson, best known for his trilogy of bouts with Floyd Patterson. The younger Johansson did not fare well in the boxing ring, losing both of her professional fights.

6. **TRACY BYRD**

Tracy Byrd, called "The Lady," is the sister of IBF world heavyweight champion Chris Byrd. Her father, Joe Byrd, a former heavyweight boxer in his own right, trains her. Tracy, a Michigan police officer, holds a record of 14–1. She began her boxing career in 1996. All of her losses have come by decision.

7. **MELISSA SALAMONE**

The sister of light heavyweight contender Lou Del Valle, Melissa "Honey Girl" Salamone has been one of the most successful female fighters in professional boxing. She has a record of 27–3–1 and has held several titles. Her brother readily acknowledges that she was the better athlete when they were young.

8. **J'MARIE MOORE**

Though less well known than many of the other fighters on this list, J'Marie Moore actually turned professional before many of the other daughters of famous champions. The daughter of the great light heavyweight champion Archie Moore, J'Marie turned pro with a victory in 1997. She has fought only one other time, earning a technical knockout in a 2000 bout. She is 2–0 as a pro.

9. CARLA (SHAKURAH) WITHERSPOON

Known as "Pugs," Shakurah Witherspoon will fight anyone at any time, which helps to explain her record of 10–34–1. She has faced the likes of Lucia Rijker, Melissa Salamone, and Tracy Byrd. She is the sister-in-law of former two-time world heavyweight champion "Terrible" Tim Witherspoon.

10. ELIZA OLSON

Eliza Olson is the granddaughter of former world middleweight champion Carl "Bobo" Olson, who won the world middleweight title in 1953. Eliza is a welterweight with a record of 6–1–1. She turned pro in 2000.

Boxers and Football

Boxing and football are two of the most violent sports. Each features a dizzying array of collisions, contusions, and concussions. Perhaps that explains the attraction to both sports for some athletes. Many boxers played football in their early days, while some football stars turned to the sport of boxing after their football careers ended—or in some cases even while they were still active on the gridiron. The following is a list of boxers who played football and football players who became boxers.

1. ED "TOO TALL" JONES

Ed "Too Tall" Jones towered over offensive linemen as a stalwart defensive end for the vaunted "Doomsday Defense" of the Dallas Cowboys in the 1970s and 1980s. Standing 6′9″, Jones harassed NFL quarterbacks with sacks and swatted passes. He shocked many, including his coach, Tom Landry, when he left the sport of football for professional boxing in 1979. His first bout was shown on national television. Jones won but could not stop an opponent nearly a foot shorter. He never lost a fight, compiling a record of 6–0. But

Jones became frustrated with boxing and returned to football with a renewed appreciation for the sport, claiming also that boxing helped him become a better football player. He may have been right, because he earned All-Pro honors after he returned to football.

2. **MARK GASTINEAU**

Mark Gastineau dominated offensive linemen as a defensive end for the New York Jets in the 1980s. Best known for his relentless pass rush, Gastineau riled the opposition by engaging in his showboating "sack dance" after sacking the quarterback. In 1985, he set an NFL record with twenty-two sacks in a single season—a record that stood until Michael Strahan of the New York Giants broke it in 2001.

Gastineau made front-page headlines for more than his boxing. He posed for *Playgirl*, dated model/movie star Brigitte Nielsen, and repeatedly ran afoul of the law. Gastineau turned to professional boxing after abruptly leaving pro football. Gastineau compiled a record of 15–2 from 1991 to 1996, although some of the results raised suspicious eyebrows. Some suspected that a few of his opponents took dives. Gastineau retired from the ring after suffering a second-round loss to fellow former NFLer Alonzo Highsmith.

3. **ALONZO HIGHSMITH**

Alonzo Highsmith was a stellar running back for the Miami Hurricanes in college. In 1987, the Houston Oilers selected him as the third overall pick in the draft. His six-year pro career was beset by injuries, and he never fulfilled the expectations that many experts had for him coming out of college. Highsmith boxed professionally from 1995 to 1998, compiling a record of 27–1–2, largely against inferior opposition. He retired from

boxing after suffering a third-round TKO loss to journeyman Terry Verners, a fighter with a record of 7–20,
and then a six-round draw against Reggie Miller.

4. LYLE ALZADO

Lyle Alzado earned fame as a great defensive lineman
for the Denver Broncos, Oakland Raiders, and Cleveland Browns. His greatest playing days were as part
of the Broncos' "Orange Crush" defense. An All-Pro,
Alzado had an equal passion for boxing. He boxed as
an amateur, compiling twenty-seven wins.

In July 1979, at the peak of his football prowess,
the never-timid Alzado fought three-time world heavyweight champion Muhammad Ali. Ali easily outpointed
Alzado in an eight-round exhibition in Denver. Sadly,
Alzado died in 1992 at the age of forty-two from brain
cancer perhaps triggered by excessive steroid use.
During his illness, Alzado spoke out about the dangers
of steroid use, admitting that he took them regularly
throughout his professional football career.

5. CHARLEY POWELL

Charley Powell played five seasons for the San Francisco 49ers and two years for the Oakland Raiders as a
defensive end, linebacker, and receiver. Powell played
high school ball in San Diego, California, but bypassed
college. Powell also pursued a career as a heavyweight
boxer. In January 1963, he squared off against Cassius
Clay, who predicted that he would stop Powell in the
third round. An ever-confident Clay said: "So, you people will believe in me, Powell must go in three." Sure
enough, Clay won in the third round. Afterward,
Powell's handlers opined that they wished he would return to football. Powell continued in boxing, retiring in
1965 with a record of 25–11–3.

6. GEORGE TRAFTON

George "The Cyclone" Trafton played college football at Notre Dame under legendary coach Knute Rockne. He also played professionally as a center for ten seasons with the Chicago Bears and was a member of the Bears' 1932 championship squad. Trafton also boxed professionally. In his biggest bout, Trafton was destroyed in the first round by Italian giant and future heavyweight champion Primo Carnera.

7. SHAZZON BRADLEY

Shazzon Bradley terrorized running backs as a defensive tackle for the University of Tennessee football team from 1988 to 1991. In the 1992 NFL draft, the Green Bay Packers selected him in the ninth round. When his professional football career did not take off, Bradley turned to the sport of boxing. From 1993 to 1999, Bradley fought twenty-one times, winning every bout. In October 1999, he captured a six-round decision over tough Sedreck Fields. During the bout, however, Bradley suffered a career-ending eye injury.

8. CHUCK DRAZENOVICH

Chuck Drazenovich won the 1950 heavyweight NCAA championship while attending Penn State. But he did not pursue a professional boxing career after college. Instead, he went to the National Football League with the Washington Redskins. Drazenovich played both offense and defense in the NFL during his first four years in the league. In his fifth year, he concentrated on the defensive side of the line as a linebacker. He earned All-Pro honors as a linebacker in 1956, 1957, and 1958.

9. KEN NORTON

Ken Norton broke Muhammad Ali's jaw in the first of their three classic bouts. He was awarded the WBC heavyweight title after champion Leon Spinks refused to fight Norton and instead gave Ali a rematch. Though Norton lost in his first title defense to Larry Holmes in a fifteen-round war, Norton was a top-notch heavyweight in one of the division's golden eras. But Norton's main sport as a young man was football. In his autobiography, *Going the Distance*, he said that in 1960, his team went undefeated and he earned all-state honors. He received more than ninety scholarship offers to play football. He chose Northeast Missouri State but suffered an injury his first year and then quit in his sophomore season. Football remained in the Norton family. His son, Ken Norton Jr., became an All-Pro linebacker for the Dallas Cowboys and the San Francisco 49ers.

10. CLIFFORD ETIENNE

Heavyweight contender Clifford Etienne had all the makings of a football star. He was a top defensive lineman for St. Martinville High School in Louisiana and attracted the attention of major college scouts. He received scholarship offers from Texas A&M, Nebraska, and Alabama before the start of his senior year. Then disaster struck.

Etienne participated in an armed robbery that ended his football career. He served nearly ten years in prison. Fortunately, Etienne discovered boxing in the joint and turned pro upon his release. He rapidly rose through the ranks of the heavyweight division, earning a victory over former Olympian Lawrence Clay-Bey. He suffered a devastating defeat at the hands of Mike Tyson in February 2003.

Boxing B-Ballers

The sports of boxing and basketball both require expert footwork. Many boxers who played basketball have credited their hoop days with providing them with good balance. Many boxers played basketball in high school and/or college before turning to the ring. Some started boxing only after finishing their b-ball careers. Others, like the great Roy Jones Jr., continue to pursue both sports.

Here is a list of ten male and female boxers who have participated in both sports.

1. ROY JONES JR.

Roy Jones Jr., perhaps the greatest pound-for-pound fighter of his generation, sometimes seems bored with boxing. Perhaps that's why one day in 1996 he made history by playing in a professional basketball game and fighting a professional prizefight in the same day. In the afternoon, he played for the Jacksonville Barracudas of the United States Basketball League (USBL), and that evening he successfully defended his super middleweight title against Eric Lucas. In 2001, Jones played some games for the USBL's Lakeland (Florida) Blue Ducks.

2. MICHAEL GRANT

Heavyweight contender Michael Grant, who stands 6'7", played power forward and center at Cal State Fullerton Junior College. He also played some football at another junior college in Texas. Grant was an undefeated contender when he faced Lennox Lewis in April 2000 for the world heavyweight title. He was stopped in the second round. After losing his next bout to Jameel McCline, he rebounded in 2002 with five straight wins. He suffered another kayo loss in 2003.

3. MARSELLES BROWN

Marselles Brown stands 6'11" and possesses a formidable left jab. Unfortunately, his chin has not stood up to the power of top-flight heavyweights. Perhaps Brown should have stayed with basketball, which he played at Springfield North High School in Ohio and briefly with Lansing Community College in Michigan. He received recruiting letters from Iowa State and the University of Detroit. He began his pro boxing career in 1989 with eleven straight wins. Then he stepped up in class slightly and was kayoed in the second round—a pattern that has continued throughout his career.

4. JAMES SPEARS

James Spears played basketball as a forward for coach John Chaney's Temple Owls from 1990 to 1992. He also played defensive end on the football team in 1993. After his collegiate career, Spears played professional basketball overseas for several years. In 2002, he launched his professional boxing career as a heavyweight. As of this writing, his record stands at 3–3.

5. JAMEEL McCLINE

Jameel "Big Time" McCline established himself as a force in the heavyweight division with wins over Michael Grant, Lance "Mount" Whitaker, and Shannon Briggs. Though he lost to Wladimir Klitschko in his last outing of 2002, McCline remains a contender for the heavyweight title. McCline, who stands 6'6", played basketball at Comsewogue High School in Port Jefferson Station, New York. According to his website, he went on to play briefly for Oneonta State University and Potsdam State before running afoul of the law.

6. TYE FIELDS

Tye "Railroad" Fields is what is known as a boxing prospect and project at the same time. His physical dimensions are imposing: 6'9" and more than 270 pounds. Before turning to boxing, Fields played college basketball at Oral Roberts and then transferred to San Diego State. In 1996, he started at power forward at San Diego State, averaging eleven points and four rebounds a game. He then played professional ball in Ireland and Russia, in addition to a stint with the Des Moines Dragons in the Continental Basketball Association (CBA). Since turning pro as a boxer, Fields has compiled a record of 29–1 with twenty-five kayoes against limited competition.

7. VONDA WARD

At 6'6", female boxing sensation Vonda Ward towers over her competition. Before her foray into boxing, Ward played four years (1992–1995) of collegiate basketball at the University of Tennessee under coach Pat Summitt. After college, Ward played pro basketball in Germany and then for the Colorado Xplosion of the now-defunct ABL. She turned pro as a boxer in January 2000 and has compiled a record of 18–0 with fourteen stoppages. She won the IBA women's heavyweight championship in December 2002.

8. FREDIA GIBBS

Nicknamed "The Cheetah," Fredia Gibbs excels in many sports. A high school track and basketball star in Pennsylvania, Gibbs earned a basketball scholarship to Temple University and then transferred to Cabrini College. After college, she went overseas and played professional basketball in Germany. When she returned to the United States in 1990, she first took up kickboxing. She reeled off sixteen straight wins and won a world title. In 1997, she began boxing and has a record of 9–2–1.

9. JACQUI FRAZIER-LYDE

Jacqui Frazier Lyde, the daughter of heavyweight great "Smokin" Joe Frazier, is an attorney and a professional boxer. Before law and boxing, Frazier-Lyde attended American University on a basketball scholarship. She made her pro debut in boxing at age thirty-eight in 2000. She has compiled a 11–1 record, losing only to Laila Ali, the daughter of Muhammad Ali.

10. JAMES "BUSTER" DOUGLAS

James "Buster" Douglas will forever be remembered as the 42–1 underdog who handed Mike Tyson his first professional defeat and captured the world heavyweight championship in 1990. The son of former light

heavyweight contender Bill "Dynamite" Douglas, the
6'4" Buster excelled at many sports in his youth, including basketball. He was a starter on the state high
school championship team in 1977 at Linden-McKinley
High School in Columbus, Ohio.

Boxing and Kickboxing

Many professional boxers turned to the ring after competing in kickboxing. The transition for some kickboxers has been difficult, as they were never able to duplicate their success in boxing. Others have become world champions. The following boxers all were kickboxers before becoming professional boxers.

1. WLADIMIR KLITSCHKO

Wladimir, the younger brother of Vitali, excelled at several sports in his youth, including kickboxing. He used his powerful legs to win championship titles six times, four times professionally and twice in the amateur ranks. But the former 1996 Olympic gold medalist is now devoted only to professional boxing. The former WBO heavyweight champion, Klitschko is seeking to rebound from an upset loss to South African Corrie Sanders in March 2003. His record stands at 41–2 with thirty-seven stoppages.

2. JAMES WARRING

James Warring was the former World Karate Association (WKA) cruiserweight champion and using only his fists won the International Boxing Federation (IBF) cruiserweight boxing championship. Warring handed kickboxing legend Bad Brad Hefton his first defeat and finished his kickboxing career with a record of 30–1–1. In 1991, Warring kayoed James Pritchard in only twenty-four seconds to win his IBF title. It was the quickest knockout ever in a world title fight. Warring finished his professional boxing career with a mark of 18–4–1.

3. TROY DORSEY

Dorsey earned his black belt in 1979 and then began professional kickboxing. Troy's first world title was won at the WAKO world championships in England in 1985. He won championships in both kickboxing and point karate. Dorsey then claimed another world title in kickboxing in 1987 and again in 1989. He captured his first boxing title in 1991, winning the IBF featherweight title in Las Vegas in a first-round knockout over Alfred Rangel. Dorsey finished with thirty-five kickboxing matches and thirty-three professional boxing matches.

4. TEX COBB

One of the most quotable men to lace up the gloves, Randall "Tex" Cobb claims to have been a North American full-contact karate champion before switching over to conventional boxing. Tex once fought a nationally televised bout, losing a nine-round decision to "Big" John Jackson for a U.S. title in the mid-1980s. He fared much better in traditional boxing, at least in terms of revenue. Said Cobb, "If I'm going to give blood, I'm going to give it to the highest bidder." Cobb parlayed his likeable tough-guy image into several acting roles.

5. RICKY HAYNES

Nicknamed "The Wolf," this Rockford, Illinois–based middleweight lost to promising middleweights John Collins and Lenny LaPaglia in the early 1980s. Haynes decided to turn his efforts to kickboxing because he said he was tired of getting fights only in opponents' backyards. Haynes never was much of a success in the boxing ring, losing many more bouts than he won. He did make a successful transition to kickboxing, winning three world titles and finishing with a record of 29–7. In between his run at kickboxing glory, Haynes sporadically competed in boxing matches, once losing a ten-round decision to former world welterweight champion Mark Breland in 1997.

6. MIKE "TENSION" NEVITT

Unlike most kickboxers who get their start in martial arts, Nevitt came up through the toughman-contest ranks, winning a light heavyweight title in 1990 in Rockford, Illinois. Nevitt went undefeated in his first twenty-one professional kickboxing bouts, capping off the run by winning a twelve-round bout for the IKF cruiserweight title in November 2002. Nevitt scored a knockout in his first professional boxing match and hopes to be a two-sport world champion.

7. ERNIE KITTERMAN

Known as "The Ironman," Ernie Kitterman of Belleville, Illinois, has won four titles fighting as a middleweight kickboxer. Kitterman is a throwback to an era when fighters stayed in top condition and didn't care who they fought. Ernie's professional boxing career hasn't fared as well as his kickboxing career. Kitterman has

Mike Nevitt

Mike "Tension" Nevitt hopes to duplicate the success he found in kickboxing in the squared circle.

competed in thirteen professional boxing matches, barely winning more than he has lost.

8. RICK "THE JET" ROUFUS

Arguably the greatest kickboxer of all time, Rick "The Jet" Roufus achieved legendary status in the sport after winning six world titles and the inaugural K-1 USA championship in 1998. Rick began martial arts at age four and rose through the national point-karate circuit, eventually defeating such legendary fighters as Steve "Nasty" Anderson. He began competing in full-contact kickboxing in his late teens. He won world titles from several sanctioning bodies in six different weight divisions. Although the thirty-two-year-old Roufus emerged victorious at the 1998 K-1 USA, things haven't gone as well for him in professional boxing. Roufus won the WBC Continental cruiserweight title but never challenged for a world title. He finished his boxing career in 2001 with a record of 13–5, losing four of his last five bouts.

9. TROY "HOLLYWOOD" HUGHES

A Rockford, Illinois, kickboxer, Hughes began his career by winning a local toughman contest and then turned his efforts toward a professional kickboxing career. He won several titles fighting throughout the United States and Europe. Hughes had only one professional boxing match, winning a decision over the lightly regarded Keith Williams in 1991.

10. KEVIN ROSIER

Rosier was a six-time world super-heavyweight kickboxing champion who has fought in every style of fighting. Rosier was a three-time WKA super-heavyweight champion and once wrestled in Japan for Antonio Inoki and the UFO (Universal Fighting-Arts Organization). In 1998, he fought in the Extreme Fight Challenge (no holds barred) competition. In 1993, he was a first-choice contender in the inaugural UFC (Ultimate Fighting Championship). Rosier's kickboxing ledger is a remarkable 66–8, but his boxing record is only 8–13. He has lost several fights by knockout, including first-round defeats to Paea Wolfgramm and Tye Fields.

Tough Man to Real Pro

The standard path for a boxer is to learn the ropes in an amateur boxing program. Once a fighter has many amateur fights, he turns pro and fights for money. However, other fighters take a different path—they fight in semipro matches called "toughman" competitions. Most toughman matches do not feature skilled boxing and proper technique. Rather, they showcase wild, crowd-pleasing brawls. Some fighters have graduated from toughman competitions into professional fighting. The following is a list of fighters who began in toughmen or toughwomen competitions and graduated to boxing with varying degrees of success.

1. BUTTERBEAN

The self-proclaimed "King of the Four-Rounders," Eric Esch, a.k.a. "Butterbean," developed a cult following after winning eighteen different titles in toughman contests and finishing as a runner-up in the national toughman tournament. He has appeared six times on *The Tonight Show* as a guest of Jay Leno and is the answer to a Trivial Pursuit question. Esch has a Sega video game named in his honor, and he is also part of another

Sega game that includes the likes of Roy Jones Jr. and Oscar De La Hoya. Esch has been featured on the undercard of several pay-per-view telecasts and continues to entertain fans with his brawling style and charismatic persona.

2. TOMMY MORRISON

While growing up in Jay, Oklahoma, Tommy "The Duke" Morrison entered the local toughman tournament at age thirteen to help support his family. After his parents divorced, Morrison worked a number of odd jobs to help his mother pay the bills. Morrison competed in toughman contests throughout Oklahoma, Missouri, and Arkansas. Morrison went on to a successful amateur boxing career, competing in several Golden Gloves tournaments before turning pro. As a professional, he captured the World Boxing Organization's (WBO) heavyweight title. He became a crowd-pleasing contender who possessed a killer left hook. Unfortunately, Morrison's career came to a halt when he announced that he was HIV-positive. He fought only once more after the diagnosis.

3. SCOTT LINDECKER

A Dubuque, Iowa, tough guy, Lindecker won several area toughman contests in the early 1980s before turning professional. Lindecker won many of his early professional bouts but faltered when he faced skilled boxers. Lindecker was featured in two Dubuque toughman contests in 1990 and 1991. He was kayoed in each event by the 7'0" Marselles "More Than a Conqueror" Brown. In 1997, he lost his last professional bout to Butterbean.

4. JOHN YOST

After winning the 1993 light-heavyweight championship at the Rockford, Illinois, toughman contest, Yost
pursued a professional boxing career. Yost's first professional bout was nationally televised on the USA Net-
work's *Tuesday Night Fights*. Billed as the "Unaboxer"
because he lived in a cabin in Northern Wisconsin that
had no running water or electricity, Yost finished his
professional career with a record of 6–2 in 2001.

5. CHRISTY MARTIN

Billed as "The Coal Miner's Daughter," Martin first
competed in toughwoman contests in West Virginia,
signing up on a dare while attending Concord College
in Athens, West Virginia. She won the event the next

John Yost

Moving from toughman competitions to boxing, John Yost (shown
here jabbing Nelson Hernandez) is billed as the "Unaboxer"
because he lives in a house with no electricity or running water.

three years. Martin went on to become a member of Don King's stable, a professional boxing champion, and one of the most famous women boxers in the history of the sport.

6. VINNY MADDALONE

While pitching minor league baseball for the Adirondack Lumberjacks in Glen Falls, New York, Maddalone entered a local toughman contest at the age of eighteen and won the heavyweight division. Maddalone won four fights on the second night of the contest to win the championship. Boxing as a pro, Vinny won his first fifteen bouts before losing by decision to former world cruiserweight champion Alfred "Ice" Cole.

7. ROCKY GANNON

An Ohio-based club fighter, Gannon began his career by winning a toughman contest and later signed a professional contract with Art Dore, one of the founders of the Original Toughman Contest. Gannon became a contender as a light heavyweight and lived and trained at Toughman headquarters in Bay City, Michigan, under the tutelage of former light heavyweight contender Murray Sutherland. He won a few fringe championship belts and finished his career with a 30–11 record.

8. ANDREA NELSON

Undefeated female boxer Andrea Nelson learned to fight in the martial arts before lacing up the gloves. Nelson won a toughwoman contest in Sault Ste. Marie in 1999 and as a professional boxer won her first seven bouts. Nelson retired undefeated from professional boxing in 2001 due to a back injury, but at the time of this writing, she is planning a return to the ring.

9. **CODY KOCH**

"The Alaskan Assassin" hailed from Anchorage and gained notoriety for his strong showing in winning fifty thousand dollars and the championship at the 1996 World Toughman Championship. Koch made rapid progress in professional boxing, winning his first twenty-four contests. Koch lost two bouts to fringe contender Ed Mahone and Wladimir Klitschko. Koch was in the process of resuming his career when he died under mysterious circumstances outside of a tavern in Shields, Michigan, in 1998. Foul play was suspected.

10. **JOHN BAILEY**

Fighting as the "Macho Midget," West Virginia's Bailey, a tough lightweight, wins most of his bouts in his native state but usually comes up short when boxing contenders in their backyard. For example, he lost decisions to Dennis Holbaek in Denmark and Ricky Hatton in Manchester, England. An accomplished All-State wrestler in high school, Bailey earned his nickname, "Macho Midget," for fighting bigger opponents in toughman competitions.

Boxer vs. Wrestler

For years boxers and wrestlers have traded barbs over who would win in the ultimate challenge for combat superiority. Many wrestlers over the years have issued public challenges to the king of the "Sweet Science"—the world heavyweight champion. Likewise, many kings of the ring have boasted that they are, to borrow Mike Tyson's phrase, "the baddest man on the planet."

Throughout the twentieth century, boxers and wrestlers have squared off in the ring with wildly inconsistent results. Heavyweight boxing legends Jack Johnson, Jack Dempsey, Joe Louis, and Muhammad Ali have all entered the ring against wrestlers. The following is a list of ten memorable bouts pitting boxer versus wrestler.

1. JACK JOHNSON VS. ANDRE SPROUL

On May 14, 1913, Johnson, the reigning heavyweight champion, was convicted of violating the "White Slave Traffic Act" in Chicago, Illinois. He was sentenced to a term of imprisonment of one year and one day, plus a fine of one thousand dollars. But instead of serving his sentence, the champion fled to Europe and engaged in boxing and wrestling matches. On November 28, 1913, he battled wrestler Andre Sproul. Johnson knocked Sproul out and a riot erupted.

2. JACK DEMPSEY VS. CLARENCE LUTTRELL

In July 1940, Jack Dempsey returned to action at the age of forty-five. Dempsey had remained active refereeing matches in boxing and wrestling. During one wrestling event in Atlanta, Georgia, on May 1, 1940, Dempsey was refereeing and got into a disagreement with wrestler Clarence "Cowboy" Luttrell during a tag-team event. The Cowboy rewrote the script, pushing Dempsey and challenging the former heavyweight champion to a fistfight. Backstage, Luttrell again angered Dempsey and the two were once again separated. The angry Dempsey then challenged Cowboy to a real contest, offering to donate his earnings to a worthy cause. Rumors surfaced that the event would be a phony affair, but Dempsey told *The New York Times*: "No. It's no gag. I'm going to fight a wrestler down in Atlanta on July 1. We're going to fight with gloves, the lightest ones Georgia officials will permit, and under Marquis of Queensbury rules. I ought to knock him out quick because I can still punch, and he doesn't know how to fight."

Those close to Dempsey were worried about the physical condition of the former champion. But Jack wasn't concerned: "Naw, I'm not takin' any chances. This Luttrell must be as old as I am. You know how those wrestlers are—they keep workin' till they're ready for the old men's home. And I know he can't fight. He swings from the floor. He's muscle-bound and slow. I don't like any part of this Luttrell and it will be a pleasure to take care of him." Luttrell hyped the event to the *Atlanta Constitution*, saying that he was "going to knock Dempsey's front teeth out" and was "dedicating himself to the task of being the man who licked Jack Dempsey." The event was a mismatch. Luttrell took three minutes of punishment in the opening round. The next round Dempsey closed the show, dropping Luttrell three times and knocking him out of the ring next to Nat Fleischer, publisher of *The Ring* magazine.

3. JOE LOUIS VS. COWBOY ROCKY LEE

Heavyweight great Joe Louis, who defended his world title twenty-five times during his eleven-year reign, chose a career in professional wrestling after retiring from boxing. Louis owed a $1-million tax debt to the government and started wrestling to earn money to pay off his debts. "It's an honorable living and it beats stealing," Louis told reporters who questioned his involvement in professional wrestling. Louis wrestled for less than a year and was injured in his bout with Lee. Louis ended up knocking the 320-pound Lee out with a forearm punch. Earlier in the contest, though, Lee jumped off the ropes and landed harder than expected on Louis's chest, breaking a few ribs in the process and causing heart damage from the force of the blow. The injury would come back to haunt Louis in later years. Louis's former adversary, Jersey Joe Walcott, was the guest referee. Cowboy Lee attempted to hurl Walcott across the ring when Jersey Joe pulled the wrestler off of Louis. Later in the contest, Walcott again attempted to separate the contestants, which gave Louis the chance to end matters with a well-placed forearm.

4. PRIMO CARNERA VS. JIM LONDOS

In 1951, former heavyweight boxing champion Primo
Carnera was a wrestler. The Italian giant battled to a
sixty-minute draw in a best-two-out-of-three falls event
with Jimmy Londos. Londos, who'd held the international heavyweight crown twenty years earlier, was
making a comeback to clean out what he called the
imposters in professional wrestling. The guest referee,
former heavyweight champion and former Carnera
conqueror Max Baer, gave the opening instructions as
if it was a boxing match. Londos won the first fall by
submission over Carnera at 39:38. Although Carnera
had a decent size advantage, Londos used leverage
and placed Carnera in the dreaded "Boston Crab" for
the submission after applying a reverse body scissors.
But Carnera took the second by applying a body scissors that forced Londos to surrender. In the third and
final fall, time expired and the contest was ruled a draw.
Carnera wrestled for a total of fourteen years and made
a decent living.

5. MUHAMMAD ALI VS. ANTONIO INOKI

This June 2, 1976, match bored fans and ended in a
fifteen-round draw at the Budokan Arena in Tokyo,
Japan. The match aired live on closed-circuit TV and
drew thirty-two thousand spectators to Shea Stadium
in New York. Inoki was forced to wear gloves (though
he removed them during the match) and was forbidden
to use any suplexes or submission holds. Inoki laid on
his back in a crablike position and kicked at Ali's legs
for much of the event. Muhammad landed only a few
meaningless jabs throughout the bout and was hospi-

talized after the match for blood clots and muscle injuries to his legs. The match was originally supposed to have had a prearranged ending, but neither party could agree on how it should end, so—rumors to the contrary notwithstanding—the match turned out to be a real (though boring) contest.

6. MIKE TYSON AT WRESTLEMANIA 14

Tyson received a reported $4 million to be an enforcer at the March 29, 1998, Wrestlemania 14 in Boston, Massachusetts, at the FleetCenter. Wrestling star Shawn Michaels figured he had it all under control when he coaxed Tyson into joining Michaels' D-Generation-X gang. But during the contest, when the regular referee became incapacitated, "Iron" Mike jumped into the ring and slapped a fast three-count on Michaels after "Stone Cold" Steve Austin laid Michaels out with his patented "Stone-Cold Stunner." When he got up, Michaels made a rush for the former boxing champion, who had switched sides and was now holding an "Austin 3:16" T-shirt. After a verbal exchange, Michaels took a swing at Tyson and missed. Tyson then landed a right hand, dropping Michaels to the canvas.

7. ARCHIE MOORE VS. MIKE DIBIASE

On March 15, 1963, Archie Moore battled wrestler "Iron" Mike DiBiase in the final fight of Moore's career. Moore had been inactive since a knockout loss to Cassius Clay six months earlier. Approaching either forty-seven or fifty, depending on who you asked, Moore agreed to "box" professional wrestler DiBiase, the father of World Wrestling Federation superstar "The Million Dollar Man" Ted DiBiase. Many in the press thought that the bout would be a fix, but that was not the case. Moore knocked out DiBiase in three rounds in a legitimate effort that went into the books as Archie's final fight.

8. **EARNIE SHAVERS**

In the early 1980s, Shavers relocated to Martinsville, Virginia, and struck up a friendship with wrestler "Big" John Studd. Studd got Shavers involved in professional wrestling as a referee. When the action in the ring became chaotic, Shavers would attempt to restore order. However, Shavers had difficulty getting the choreography down as he noted in his autobiography, *Welcome to the Big Time*: "Backstage before each match, I would work backstage with the wrestler I was going to 'KO' later, rehearsing the big blow. The trick in these situations is to pull back your fist the second you feel the chin of the other guy." But it didn't always work out that way for the heavy-handed Shavers. "When you've been whacking people on the chin as long as I had and meaning it, going the other way took some getting used to," wrote Shavers. Earnie followed through with one too many blows during his brief professional career and soon found himself out of wrestling.

9. **SCOTT LEDOUX VS. LARRY ZBYSKO**

On April 20, 1986, former wrestling great Verne Gagne, founder of the American Wrestling Association (AWA), promoted an event at the Metrodome in Minneapolis, Minnesota, that attracted twenty-two thousand fans. The main event pitted former heavyweight boxing challenger Scott LeDoux of Minnesota against the brash, outspoken AWA wrestling great Zbysko in a boxing match. Zbysko was the self-proclaimed "Living Legend" of wrestling and boasted that he personally had run his former mentor Bruno Sammartino out of the sport. LeDoux had become a referee for the AWA after his boxing career had ended and had started a feud with Zbysko. Finally it was to be settled in the ring with both combatants wearing karate gloves. The first two rounds were uneventful until Larry the Legend landed a few cheap shots near the end of the second round. Zbysko resumed his dirty tactics in the next stanza. But in round four, LeDoux mounted a comeback and pounded Zbysko all over the ring, knocking the grappler out cold at the bell. After Zbysko was saved by the bell, the action moved to the floor outside the ring. Both contestants were disqualified for their combat outside the ring.

10. CHUCK WEPNER VS. ANDRE THE GIANT

On June 25, 1976, in Shea Stadium, New York, boxer Chuck Wepner faced the behemoth Andre the Giant. Wepner, a 225-pound ex-Marine from Bayonne, New Jersey, was known for his sturdy chin and easily cut face. Wepner had challenged Muhammad Ali the previous year and in the ninth round had knocked the champion down with a right to the chest, although photos later showed that he was stepping on Ali's foot when he hit him. But now Wepner was challenging a much larger opponent—the 7'4", 500-pound giant billed as "The Eighth Wonder of the World." Andre dominated the match, and Wepner was eventually hurled outside the ring. Wepner was unable to get back into the ring and was counted out in the third round.

Highly Educated Boxers

Too much credence is given to the stereotype that boxers are all brawn and no brains. Nothing could be further from the truth. Take the example of former world champion Bobby Czyz, who is a member of Mensa—a group composed of people with IQs greater than 140. The following is a list of boxers who obtained a bachelor's degree or higher in their pursuit of education. While one does not need a college degree to be intelligent, these boxers have shown that one can excel at both athletics and academics.

1. WLADIMIR KLITSCHKO

Heavyweight sensation Wladimir Klitschko, holder of the WBO world heavyweight title, also holds a Ph.D. in sports science from the University of Kiev. He earned this advanced degree in June 2001. Wladimir appeared on a fast track to meet recognized champion Lennox Lewis until a shocking upset kayo loss at the hands of Corrie Sanders in March 2003. Klitschko, the younger brother of Vitali (who is also highly educated) sports a record of 41–2.

2. CARLOS PALOMINO

Mexican-born Carlos Palomino won the WBC world welterweight championship in 1976 and then defended his crown seven times. Palomino also earned a college degree from California State University in Long Beach in 1976. He became the first world champion boxer to hold a college degree. Palomino retired in 1979 and made a ring comeback in 1997. He won four fights before losing a ten-round decision. His career record was 31–4–3, and he was never knocked out in the ring. He has enjoyed a successful acting career.

3. JAMES "BONECRUSHER" SMITH

James "Bonecrusher" Smith became the first world heavyweight champion with a college degree when he knocked out "Terrible" Tim Witherspoon in the first round in December 1986 for the WBA belt. Smith earned a degree in business administration from Shaw University in Raleigh, North Carolina. Smith fought from 1981 to 1999, compiling a record of 44–17–1.

4. GUTY ESPADAS JR.

Guty Espadas Jr. won the WBC featherweight championship in 2000. He defended his crown once before dropping a disputed decision to Erik Morales. Espadas, the son of a former world champion, was pushed by his father to pursue his education. He earned a college degree in engineering from the University of Merida, Mexico. He continues to pursue a second world title.

5. WILLIE DE WIT

Canada's Willie de Wit won a silver medal at the 1984 Los Angeles Olympic Games as a heavyweight. He turned pro and compiled a record of 20–1–1. His only loss was by kayo to power-punching Bert Cooper. In his last fight, de Wit decisioned Henry Tillman, the man who'd defeated him for the gold medal. De Wit not only earned a college degree from Grande Prairie Regional College, but upon retirement he obtained a law degree from the University of Alberta.

6. DAVARRYL WILLIAMSON

Heavyweight contender Davarryl "Touch of Sleep" Williamson is far from the typical boxer. For one, he did not begin his amateur boxing career until he was twenty-five. Secondly, he earned a bachelor of science degree from Wayne State University in Nebraska and a master's degree in administrative services from Northern Michigan University. He has a professional boxing record of 18–2 with sixteen kayoes.

7. CHUCK DAVEY

Chuck Davey, a popular television boxer in the 1950s, was a ranked welterweight contender who held victories over Rocky Graziano, Carmen Basilio, and Ike Williams. A four-time NCAA boxing champion at Michigan State, he turned pro and became a fan favorite on television. He lost in his only world title attempt to Cuban great Kid Gavilan in February 1953. Davey earned a bachelor's degree and a master's from MSU.

8. AUDLEY HARRISON

British heavyweight prospect Audley Harrison hopes to capture a world title in the professional ranks. Harrison rose to prominence by winning the gold medal at super heavyweight at the 2000 Olympic Games in Sydney, Australia. Harrison, who served more than eighteen months in prison in his youth, turned his life around through education. From 1992 to 1995, he attended the College of North-East London, earning a degree.

9. ARMAND EMANUEL

San Francisco–based Armand Emanuel was a light heavyweight contender in the late 1920s who was also a practicing lawyer at the time he was boxing. He lost a disputed decision to 175-pound king Tommy Lough-ran in a nontitle bout in 1928 and was considered a surefire future champion until being derailed by Mickey "The Toy Bulldog" Walker.

10. HENRY MILLIGAN

Henry Milligan was a cruiserweight prospect in the 1980s known for his crowd-pleasing style. Milligan lost in the semifinals of the 1984 Olympic trials to none other than Mike Tyson. Milligan turned pro and won his first eleven bouts by knockout. However, he was stopped twice in 1986. He also lost via kayo in a comeback in the 1990s. Milligan earned a civil engineering degree from Princeton University. He later obtained a master's in business administration (MBA) from New York University. He also is a member of Mensa, a group of people with high IQs.

Boxers/Referees

R etirement has been a difficult adjustment for many fighters. The adulation they receive in the ring cannot easily be replaced in life without boxing. Perhaps for this reason, many fighters stay in the fight game as trainers, managers, cutmen, or referees. Many boxers have become the so-called third man in the ring upon their retirement. Other fighters, particularly earlier in the twentieth century, refereed fights during the prime of their careers. Still other fighters had mediocre or short professional careers as boxers but achieved greater success as referees.

Here are ten individuals who both boxed and refereed professionally.

1. JAMES J. JEFFRIES

James J. Jeffries retired as undefeated heavyweight champion in 1904. Before his ill-fated comeback to reclaim the throne from Jack Johnson in 1910, Jeffries served as a referee at his athletic club in Vernon, California. On September 7, 1908, he refereed the world championship rematch between middleweight greats Billy Papke and Stanley Ketchel.

2. JERSEY JOE WALCOTT

Jersey Joe Walcott, born Arnold Cream, became heavyweight champion at the age of thirty-seven in 1951. Though he lost his title in his second defense to Rocky Marciano in a classic bout, Walcott is still considered one of the best boxers of his era. Walcott refereed numerous important bouts after he retired in 1953. Perhaps most noteworthy, he was the third man in the rematch between Cassius Clay and Sonny Liston, a bout that ended somewhat mysteriously in the first round. Walcott later became chairman of the New Jersey Athletic Commission.

3. WILLIE PEP

Willie Pep was a master boxer perennially listed by most experts as one of the ten greatest fighters of all time. Called the "Will O' the Wisp" for his remarkable defensive abilities, he once reputedly won a round without throwing a single punch. After his ring career finally ended, Pep refereed many bouts. In 1969, Pep was the referee and sole judge of the world featherweight championship bout between Fighting Harada and Johnny Famechon. Pep initially scored the bout a draw, but it was discovered he had incorrectly added the totals. He actually scored the bout for Famechon, even though most experts thought Harada had won the fight.

4. RICHARD STEELE

Richard Steele was a tough light heavyweight from Los Angeles, California, who fought in the late 1960s. He compiled a respectable record of 16–4, though he never fought for a world title. Steele made his mark in boxing as a top-flight referee, working more than 160 world title bouts. He refereed the first Sugar Ray Leonard–Thomas Hearns and the Sugar Ray Leonard–Marvelous Marvin Hagler bouts. He currently manages fighters.

5. MILLS LANE

Mills Lane is best known for his no-nonsense style of refereeing and his trademark phrase "Let's Get It On!" which he said to fighters at the beginning of a bout. Lane sported a 45–4 record as an amateur, winning an NCAA boxing title at the University of Nevada-Reno. He nearly made the 1960 Olympic boxing team. He turned pro in 1961 and lost his pro debut but rebounded to post a career ledger of 11–1. Then, as he says in his autobiography, appropriately entitled *Let's Get It On*, he turned in his "boxing trunks for bow ties." Lane refereed many top world championship fights including Larry Holmes–Ken Norton, Mike Tyson–Evander Holyfield II, and Holmes–Gerry Cooney.

6. GEORGES CARPENTIER

Georges Carpentier was a former world light heavyweight champion and heavyweight contender who fought in every pro division from flyweight to heavyweight. This popular Frenchman unsuccessfully challenged Jack Dempsey for the world heavyweight title in 1921. Eight years earlier, in 1913, the twenty-year-old Carpentier served as the third man in the ring for the bout between then-heavyweight champion Jack Johnson and Andre Sproul held in Paris. In 1914, he also refereed Johnson's title defense against Frank Moran.

7. BENNY LEONARD

Many boxing historians consider Benny Leonard as the greatest lightweight of all time. He held the world title in that division from 1917 to 1923 and fought more than two hundred bouts in a twenty-one-year-career. He lost only five bouts in his entire career. Leonard refereed many bouts after his ring career. He died in 1947 of a heart attack while refereeing a six-round bout between Mario Ramon and Bobby Williams at St. Nicholas Arena in New York.

8. JOE JEANETTE

Joe Jeanette was a great, early African-American boxer denied a shot at the world title because of the color line. Even Jack Johnson, the first African-American heavyweight champ, would not fight Jeanette when he became champion. After his long ring career, Jeanette stayed in boxing and worked as a referee.

9. RUBY GOLDSTEIN

Ruby Goldstein, known as "The Jewel of the Ghetto," was a former professional fighter whose claim to fame came not as a boxer but as a referee. Goldstein won his first twenty-three fights but was stopped in his biggest fights. He suffered a kayo loss to Hall of Famer Jimmy McLarnin. Goldstein, who began refereeing at age thirty-four, worked many world title fights, including Joe Louis–Jersey Joe Walcott, Joey Maxim–Sugar Ray Robinson, and the tragic Emile Griffith–Benny Paret bout in which Paret died.

10. ARTHUR DONOVAN

Arthur Donovan is the son of American middleweight great Mike Donovan and the father of ex-Baltimore

Colts football player Art Donovan. He achieved lasting fame as a referee in the 1920s, 1930s, and 1940s. Donovan refereed numerous Joe Louis bouts, including both of his fights against German great Max Schmeling. Donovan fought as a professional under an assumed name to avoid the disapproval of his father, who did not want his son to box.

Boxing Musicians

Many boxers have turned their attention to more than just the rigorous training demanded of a well-conditioned athlete in the ring. Others have sought glamour, attention, or personal satisfaction in playing music. Whether rap, pop, or country, boxers have turned to various genres of music to fulfill their dreams and desires. For example, legendary Motown recording artist Marvin Gaye used to spar regularly with professional boxer Tom Hanna. The following boxers have plied or are plying their craft in the music business. Others on this list boxed in their youth before making music their number-one priority. Some were world champions, others no more than journeymen. But they all shared a profound love of music.

1. ROY JONES JR.

Roy Jones Jr., the man many consider to be boxing's current pound-for-pound best, has dabbled in the music genre of rap. His first album, called *Round One*, featured hit songs such as "That Was Then" and "Y'all Must Have Forgot"—a song apparently aimed toward the boxer's critics who forgot that he had faced several top fighters in his career.

2. OSCAR DE LA HOYA

Oscar De La Hoya, "The Golden Boy," has won Olympic gold and numerous pro world titles in various weight divisions. For a brief period, De La Hoya turned his attention from the ring to another childhood love—music. De La Hoya made an album, appropriately entitled *Oscar*. One hit song on his album, "Ven a Mi," earned a Latin Grammy nomination. In 2000, De La Hoya married Latin pop singer Millie Corretjer.

3. LIONEL ROSE

Lionel Rose was born in the aboriginal settlement Jackson Tract in Australia in 1948. He turned pro after a successful amateur career. In 1968, he traveled to Tokyo, Japan, to face the legendary Masahiko "Fighting" Harada for the world bantamweight crown. Rose won a fifteen-round decision. He lost his title the next year to Ruben Olivares. Rose turned to music in the 1970s, including a collaboration with musician Laurie Allen on the album *Jackson Tracts*.

4. JOE FRAZIER

"Smokin" Joe Frazier was an Olympic gold medalist and world heavyweight champion best known for his trilogy with the great Muhammad Ali. With his trademark left hook and relentless attack, Frazier kayoed many opponents. During the latter part of his boxing career and afterward, Frazier played with a band called The Knockouts. His talent for singing did not match his boxing prowess.

5. **LARRY HOLMES**

Larry Holmes was one of the greatest heavyweight champions in history, with one of the greatest left jabs the division has ever seen. When he retired from the ring (for the first time) after successive losses to Michael Spinks, Holmes toured the country with a seven-man band called Marmalade. He sang with the group at gigs across the country. In 1987, he and Joe Frazier were invited to perform in Atlantic City during the week of the Michael Spinks–Gerry Cooney fight.

6. **WILLIE DIXON**

Blues music devotees will remember the name of Willie Dixon, who performed and wrote many leading blues songs in the 1940s. He wrote such songs as "Hoochie Coochie Man" and "I Just Want to Make Love to You" for fellow blues great Muddy Waters. He played in bands called The Five Breezes, The Four Jumps of Five, and The Big Three Trio. But before he became a blues great, Dixon was a boxer. In 1937, he won the Illinois Golden Gloves championship in the heavyweight division. He turned pro but had only four bouts.

7. **ERNIE TERRELL**

Ernie Terrell was a top heavyweight contender for much of the 1960s who lost to Muhammad Ali by fifteen-round decision for the world title in 1967. Terrell's band, Ernie Terrell and the Knockouts, once made an appearance on *The Tonight Show*. One of the members of the band was Terrell's sister, Jean, who in 1969 replaced the great Diana Ross as a member of The Supremes. Ernie had invited Motown founder Berry Gordy to watch the band perform. Gordy was so impressed with Jean that he asked her to join The Supremes.

8. ROBERT DIXON

Robert Dixon was involved with boxing nearly his entire adult life as a boxer, trainer, and coach. He had more than one hundred professional pro bouts and served as a sparring partner to world featherweight champion Sandy Saddler. Dixon left the ring to become a member of the Nashville, Tennessee, recording group The Neptunes. Dixon died at the age of sixty-nine in August 2002.

9. MILTON WYNN

Milton Wynn is an up-and-coming heavyweight who nearly made the 1996 Olympic team with an impressive amateur record of 22–1. Wynn has compiled a pro record of 8–0 against relatively weak opposition. Wynn, along with the gospel group Decision, recorded a critically acclaimed album entitled *Time to Pull Together*.

10. MIKE RODGERS

Mike Rodgers, nicknamed the "Honky Tonk Hitman," captured the World Boxing Federation's super cruiserweight title in October 2002 with a second-round stoppage over Art Jimmerson. But Rodgers possesses more talent as an aspiring country musician than as a boxer. Popular on the club circuit, Rodgers has opened for such legends as Merle Haggard and David Allan Coe. He often plays at a popular spot in Nashville, Tennessee, a.k.a. "Country Music, U.S.A.," called Legends.

Stacy Allen

Mike Rodgers, "The Honky Tonk Hitman," packs a wallop with both
his fists and his voice.

Heavyweights in Hollywood

Most casual boxing fans pay attention mostly to heavyweights. Hollywood filmmakers have been no different, as many heavyweights have obtained greater attention from the cinematic world than their lighter counterparts. The following former heavyweight boxers all turned in their ring gloves for a shot at the silver screen.

1. RANDALL "TEX" COBB

Former title challenger Cobb has carved out a second career in Tinseltown. He has appeared in more than twenty movies including: *The Golden Child*, *Uncommon Valor*, *Raising Arizona*, *Diggstown*, and *The Naked Gun 33 1/3: The Final Insult*. Cobb has also appeared on the following television series: *Miami Vice*, *Hardcastle and McCormick*, *Married . . . With Children*, and *MacGyver*.

2. VICTOR MCLAGLEN

Great Britain's Victor McLaglen fought exhibition bouts with heavyweight champions Bob Fitzsimmons and Jack Johnson in 1909. McLaglen lived a full life, working at various times as a policeman, circus strongman, and professional wrestler. He also acted in several movies, including the lead role in the 1935 film *The Informer*, which earned him a "Best Actor" Oscar. He also starred in *The Beloved Brute*, *What Price Glory?* and *Klondike Annie*.

3. EARNIE SHAVERS

After catching Sylvester Stallone with a crunching body punch in a film audition, Shavers blew an opportunity to star as Clubber Lang in *Rocky III*. Stallone later told Shavers that he doubted if the viewing public would buy into him defeating Shavers on the big screen. Years later, Shavers received his chance in the movies, appearing as himself in a bit part in *Honeymoon in Las Vegas*. Years earlier, Earnie appeared on the set for *Smokey and the Bandit II,* but his part was edited out of the movie.

4. JACK O'HALLORAN

This former heavyweight contender went undefeated in his first sixteen bouts before turning into a journeyman who lost to such world-class fighters as George Foreman, Joe Bugner, and Ken Norton. O'Halloran met Steve McQueen while the actor was shooting *The Thomas Crown Affair* in Boston but turned down a chance to appear in the film to concentrate on his boxing career. Later, O'Halloran had roles in *Superman I* and *II*, *The Flintstones*, *King Kong*, and *Farewell, My Lovely*. O'Halloran has also made guest appearances on *Murder She Wrote* and *Knight Rider*.

5. BOBBY HITZ

Former heavyweight boxer and current Chicago premier boxing promoter Bobby Hitz fought George Foreman and Craig "The Gator" Bodzianowski during his professional career. Although busy trying to return to boxing in Chicago to its glory years, Hitz found time to play an enforcer in the crime drama *The Deal*, which was shot on scene in Chicago.

6. MAX BAER

Heavyweight champion Max Baer, "The Clown Prince of Boxing," made his cinematic debut in the 1933 movie *The Prizefighter and the Lady*, which starred Myrna Loy. Baer played roles in more than twenty motion pictures and also had a guest appearance on *The Lone Ranger* playing a foreman named Sampson. Baer's son, Max Jr., went on to fame starring as Jethro on *The Beverly Hillbillies*.

7. GEORGE FOREMAN

Big George Foreman started appearing in sitcoms during his first championship reign in the early 1970s. He made appearances on *The Six Million Dollar Man* and *Sanford and Son*. In 1993, during his second career as a professional boxer, Foreman starred in his own sitcom, *George*. But Foreman's popularity didn't cross over enough into the mainstream, and the show was canceled after only ten episodes.

8. JAMES TILLIS

James "Quick" Tillis lost a decision to Mike Weaver in 1981 for the WBA world heavyweight championship. He is also known as the first man to go the distance with Mike Tyson when Tyson was an undefeated human destroyer. Tillis appeared in the Oscar-winning movie *The Color Purple* alongside Oprah Winfrey in 1985 and later received a role in *Percy & Thunder*, a

1993 film about a retired boxer and his protégé entering the big-time world of boxing, starring James Earl
Jones.

9. KEN NORTON

Heavyweight champion Ken Norton received his first
starring role as a bare knuckle–fighting slave in the
1975 movie *Mandingo* and then was featured a year
later as another muscle-flexing slave in *Drum*. Norton
also appeared as a prisoner in an episode of the television hit series *The A-Team*. The former champion's last
acting role was as a security guard in the 1998 movie
Frog and Wombat.

10. MUHAMMAD ALI

"The Greatest" played himself in the movie of his life,
The Greatest, based on his autobiography written with
Richard Durham. The 1977 movie features such prominent performers as Robert Duvall, Pam Grier, and
James Earl Jones. Ali played the lead role in the 1979
movie *Freedom Road* with Kris Kristofferson. During his
exile from the ring for refusing induction into the draft
for the Vietnam War, Ali appeared in the Broadway mu-
sical *Buck White*.

Top Boxing Movies

Boxing has long attracted the attention of film-makers, perhaps because of the inherent action of fistic competition or the legions of legendary ring warriors or maybe the seedy side of the "Sweet Science." Whatever the reason, no one can question that boxing has produced many great films. The following is a list of ten of the best boxing movies ever made.

1. **ROCKY (1976)**

Sylvester Stallone's portrayal of a down-and-out club fighter named Rocky Balboa who gets a shot at the heavyweight title when a top contender can't be found on short notice was named "Best Picture" at the 1976 Academy Awards. Rocky makes the best of his limited skills to become the first person to go the distance with heavyweight champion Apollo Creed and proves to himself that he is not a "bum," in the words of his irascible trainer, played by Burgess Meredith. Rocky loses the decision in the title bout but wins over pet-store clerk Adrian in one of the greatest sports movies ever made. The scene in which Rocky drinks raw eggs is a classic etched in the minds, if not stomachs, of every *Rocky* fan.

2. BODY AND SOUL (1947)

This is the story of a middleweight boxer who must make difficult choices on his way to the title when dealing with shady promoters. The story centers on boxer Charley Davis, played by John Garfield, who began fighting to save himself and his mother from hardship after his dad was killed in a mob-related incident. This movie was nominated for three Academy Awards. A 1981 version of this movie starring Leon Isaac Kennedy in the lead role was also popular.

3. REQUIEM FOR A HEAVYWEIGHT (1962)

This movie depicts the story of boxer Mountain Rivera, played by Anthony Quinn, who is facing the end of his career. The story deals with the corruption in boxing, including fight fixing and gambling. This film is loosely based on the life of former heavyweight champion Primo Carnera, who, like Mountain Rivera, was forced into professional wrestling to make a living.

4. FAT CITY (1972)

This drama starring Stacey Keach and Jeff Bridges explores the relationship between a former main-eventer, played by Keach, and his young protégé, played by Bridges. It is a depressing movie that powerfully depicts the tough world of professional boxing in Stockton, California. Keach's character makes a ring comeback that goes nowhere. The movie displays the sad confusion experienced by a former fighter who ineffectively deals with life outside of boxing.

5. **THE HARDER THEY FALL (1956)**

This movie stars Humphrey Bogart in his last role. He plays an unemployed sportswriter who helps build up a harmless Argentine giant, Tono Molina, into a heavyweight sensation and suffers pangs of conscience along the way as the mob bleeds Molina dry. Bogart died soon after filming. The movie features performances by former heavyweight champions Max Baer and Jersey Joe Walcott.

6. **THE QUIET MAN (1952)**

John Wayne plays an American boxer named Sean Thornton who returns to his birthplace in Ireland, called White O'Mornin' in the town of Inisfree, to regroup after killing a man in the ring. Thornton's troubles begin when village tough guy Will Danaher, played by former professional boxer Victor McLaglen (who once fought former heavyweight champions Jack Johnson and Bob Fitzsimmons in exhibitions), takes exception to Thornton's romance with his sister, played by Maureen O'Hara. The climax of this John Wayne classic is a fistfight between Thornton and Danaher that ranges all over the village.

7. **RAGING BULL (1980)**

This vivid biography of former middleweight champion Jake LaMotta portrays the violent nature that almost destroyed him. Shot in black and white to emphasize the bleakness of the story, the film follows LaMotta from early in his career to about a decade after his retirement. Joe Pesci as LaMotta's brother, Joey, gives a great performance nearly equal to Robert De Niro's stunning portrayal of LaMotta, for which he received a "Best Actor" Oscar.

8. SOMEBODY UP THERE LIKES ME (1956)

This movie chronicles the transformation of street-thug Thomas Rocco Barbella to Rocky Graziano, middleweight champion of the world. Paul Newman stars as Graziano. In the early scenes, Steve McQueen appears as one of Graziano's hoodlum friends. The movie covers Graziano's turbulent relationship with his father, who had yearned to be a boxer himself. It also tells Rocky's rags-to-riches story of going from dishonorable dischargee from the armed services to world champion. Graziano's real-life arch rival in the ring, Tony Zale, plays himself in the movie.

9. GENTLEMAN JIM (1942)

Errol Flynn stars as James J. "Gentleman Jim" Corbett in one of his top performances. Ward Bond plays Corbett's nemesis, John L. Sullivan, and is also outstanding. The film centers on Corbett, the first world heavyweight champion under the new Marquis of Queensberry rules. His defeat of Sullivan, the legendary "Boston Strong Boy," is ring folklore. This movie is difficult to find but well worth the effort.

10. THE CHAMP (1931)

This movie stars Wallace Beery as a former heavyweight champion and struggling alcoholic who relies on the strength of his son's love to carry him to redemption. The sentimental movie garnered Beery a "Best Actor" Oscar and won for best original story. A 1979 version of the movie featured Jon Voight as the former champion and Ricky Schroeder as his adoring son.

Real Boxing Personalities in the Reel *Rocky* Saga

Sylvester Stallone became inspired to write his classic story of Rocky Balboa, a journeyman-turned-world title contender, after watching the outmatched Chuck Wepner courageously battle Muhammad Ali in 1975. The result was an Oscar-winning film called *Rocky*. The movie became madly popular with the public and led to four sequels. There is talk that there may even be a Rocky VI in the works.

While Stallone is not a real boxer, the *Rocky* movies do contain many real-life boxers in various parts. The following are ten boxers or boxing officials who appeared in one or more of the movies.

1. ROBERTO DURAN

If you blinked you would have missed Roberto "Hands of Stone" Duran in the ring sparring with the "Italian Stallion." Duran's character in the movie was shown briefly sparring with Rocky preparing him for the big fight with heavyweight champion Apollo Creed, played by Carl Weathers. Duran was one of the greatest lightweight champions in the history of boxing who also gained fame by winning the world welterweight title from Sugar Ray Leonard.

2. PEDRO LOVELL

Former 1970s fringe contender Pedro Lovell may be best known for almost losing his toupee in a knockout loss to Ken Norton. Lovell came from an Argentine fighting family, as his father, Alberto Santiago Lovell, had once fought Archie Moore in 1951 in Argentina. Pedro had done most of his professional fighting in California and landed a small role as a club fighter in the original *Rocky* movie. Lovell appears in the first scene as club fighter Spider Rico. The scene occurs in a dark arena, with both combatants fighting beneath a giant painting of Jesus. The spectators boo both boxers for clinching until Rico purposely butts Rocky and opens up a gash on Balboa's eye. This riles up our hero, who dispatches Rico to another defeat.

3. TOMMY MORRISON

Tommy "The Duke" Morrison, the former WBO heavyweight champion, played Rocky Balboa's protégé, Tommy "Machine" Gunn, in *Rocky V*. Gunn later turns against Balboa, forcing the ex-champion to put the youngster in his place. The movie, coupled with Morrison's good looks and powerful left hook, catapulted him to boxing stardom. Unfortunately, an HIV diagnosis effectively ended his career.

4. STAN WARD

Former California state heavyweight champion Stan Ward, who fought out of Sacramento, finished his professional career with a record of 21–7–2. Ward lost to onetime heavyweight champions Greg Page, Mike

Weaver, and Gerrie Coetzee in his career. Ward appeared as one of the nameless contenders knocked out by Tommy Morrison's character, Tommy Gunn, in *Rocky V*.

5. MIKE WILLIAMS

Former fringe heavyweight contender Mike Williams retired in 2000 with a record of 22–6. During his career he lost to former heavyweight champions Tim Witherspoon and Buster Douglas. Williams never reached his potential to be world champ in real life, but in *Rocky V*, he played the character of Union Cane, world heavyweight champion. In the movie Cane is knocked out by Rocky's protégé, Tommy Gunn (Tommy Morrison), and loses his heavyweight title. Morrison and Williams were once scheduled to box each other in the pro ranks for Morrison's WBO crown, but the match never materialized, reportedly because Williams refused to take a drug test.

6. AL SILVANI

Al Silvani trained Hall of Fame fighters Rocky Graziano, Jake LaMotta, and Alexis Arguello. He gave boxing lessons to entertainer Frank Sinatra and actor Clint Eastwood, with whom he appeared in several movies. Al spent most of his days as a trainer in the famed Stillman's Gym in New York. Silvani was a "cut man" in the first three movies of the *Rocky* series and even got to use his real name.

7. EDDIE "THE ANIMAL" LOPEZ

Los Angeles–based heavyweight Lopez won his first ten professional fights and finished his career in 1984 with a record of 22–4. He lost fights to former champions

"Big" John Tate and Tony Tucker and to contender Gerry Cooney. In 1980, he fought Leon Spinks to a ten-round draw. Lopez made a brief appearance in *Rocky II* as a boxer. In the credits Lopez is listed merely as a "fighter."

8. LOU FILLIPO

Championship boxing referee Lou Fillipo appeared in all five *Rocky* movies as a referee of several of Rocky Balboa's title bouts. Fillipo works many shows in the Southern California area and was a professional fighter before becoming a judge and referee.

9. TONY BURTON

Former professional boxer Tony Burton played Apollo Creed's head trainer, Duke. Tony was a light heavyweight in the late 1950s in Southern California who did most of his boxing in Hollywood and Los Angeles. Knockout specialist Lamar Clark stopped Burton on April 4, 1960, in Palm Springs, California. Burton fared much better acting in Hollywood than he did fighting there, appearing in the first four films in the *Rocky* saga.

10. "SMOKIN" JOE FRAZIER

Who can forget the former world heavyweight champion Joe Frazier greeting Rocky and champion Apollo Creed in the ring before the climatic championship fight? In the movie, Creed tells Frazier that he's next. Frazier, the real-life Philadelphia heavyweight great, was on hand for the birth of the greatest fictional fighter to hail from the City of Brotherly Love.

Boxing Figures in the Movie *Ali*

In 2001, boxing fans were treated to an impressive film on the life and career of the great Muhammad Ali, appropriately entitled *Ali*. Former rap superstar Will "The Fresh Prince" Smith portrayed Ali, while comedian/actor Jamie Foxx stole scenes as Ali exhorter Drew "Bundini" Brown. Jon Voight also gave a fine performance as the legendary, pompous announcer Howard Cosell. The fight scenes were made more authentic by having Smith square off against real boxers. The following is a list of boxers and boxing officials who played roles in the movie.

1. JAMES TONEY

James "Lights Out" Toney is a former middleweight and super middleweight world champion who currently seeks a world cruiserweight title. He won the IBF world middleweight title in 1991 with a come-from-behind kayo of the talented Michael Nunn. Then, in 1993, he captured the IBF super middleweight crown with a win over the rugged Iran Barkley. Toney received rave reviews for his performance as "Smokin" Joe Frazier in the movie.

2. CHARLES SHUFFORD

A fringe heavyweight contender, Charles Shufford played George Foreman in the movie. Shufford is a good boxer who holds wins over Jimmy Thunder, Lamon Brewster, and Eliecer Castillo. As of October 2003, his record stood at 20–4.

3. ALFRED COLE

Alfred "Ice" Cole is a former world cruiserweight champion. He captured the IBF world cruiserweight title in 1992 and made five successful defenses before moving up to heavyweight. In the movie, he portrays Ali opponent and former WBA heavyweight champion Ernie Terrell. He has a record of 34–11–3.

4. MICHAEL BENTT

Michael Bentt is a former WBO world heavyweight champion who portrays former world heavyweight champion Sonny Liston in the movie. The unheralded Bentt shocked the boxing world by stopping Tommy Morrison in the first round to win the title in 1993. He lost to Herbie Hide via seventh-round knockout in his first defense. Bentt retired after that loss with a record of 11–2.

5. LARRY HAZZARD SR.

New Jersey Boxing Commissioner Larry Hazzard Sr., a former world-class referee, plays referee Zack Clayton in the movie. Clayton was the referee of the Muhammad Ali–George Foreman bout in Zaire. Hazzard was appointed New Jersey commissioner in 1985. His son is now a well-known boxing judge.

6. **MARTY DENKIN**

Marty Denkin is an experienced ring official from California who has refereed and judged numerous world title bouts. In the movie, Denkin plays the ring announcer of the second Ali–Frazier bout. Denkin is no stranger to boxing movies. He played a Russian referee in *Rocky IV*.

7. **ROBERT BYRD**

Robert Byrd is a world-class referee who has worked more than fifty world championship title fights. A former law enforcement officer, Byrd has worked bouts in both California and Nevada. In the movie he portrays Willie Reddish, a cornerman for heavyweight champion Sonny Liston.

8. **DERRICK BROWN**

Heavyweight prospect Derrick "D-Train" Brown portrays former world champion Larry Holmes in the movie. Brown has a record of 11–2–1, losing his last fight of 2002 to fellow prospect Jean-Francois Bergeron.

9. **DAMIEN WILLS**

Heavyweight boxer Damien "Bolo" Wills portrays former world champion Ken Norton in the movie. Wills made his professional boxing debut in February 2002, winning by third-round knockout.

10. **JAMES GILBERT**

Journeyman heavyweight James Gilbert from Zimbabwe portrays a sparring partner for Ali in the movie, helping Ali prepare for George Foreman in Zaire. Gilbert has a record of 6–5–1 and has lost his last five bouts.

Named by Ali

The greatest showman in boxing history was none other than Muhammad Ali, "The Greatest." Ali learned the art of self-promotion from wrestler Gorgeous George, who would parade around the ring in fancy costumes making lofty boasts. Ali picked up quickly the art of prefight hype and often dubbed his opponents with humorous nicknames.

1. THE GORILLA

Muhammad Ali called his arch rival Joe Frazier "The Gorilla" before their rubber match—the so-called Thrilla in Manila. During the prefight hype, Ali pulled out a black rubber toy gorilla and began pounding it, saying: "Come on gorilla; we're in Manila. Come on gorilla; this is a thrilla."

2. THE MUMMY

Ali labeled George Foreman a "mummy," saying that Big George was slow as one. "He moves like a slow mummy, and there ain't no mummy gonna whip the great Muhammad Ali." To the amazement of many, Ali whipped the favored Foreman in their 1974 "Rumble in the Jungle," employing his famous "rope-a-dope" strategy to let Foreman punch himself out before Ali finished him in the eighth round.

3. THE BEAR

Cassius Clay taunted heavyweight champion Sonny Liston, hoping to lure the feared champion into a title bout. Clay called Liston a "big, ugly bear." "Liston is a tramp; I am the champ. I want that big ugly bear." He even drove to Liston's house in Denver, Colorado, in his bus, taunting the champion. Oddsmakers pegged Liston as a seven-to-one favorite to beat the brash young challenger, but on February 24, 1964, Cassius Clay "shook up the world" when he defeated Liston to win the title.

4. THE RABBIT

Ali dubbed Floyd Patterson, the former two-time heavyweight champion, a "rabbit," saying that Patterson was "scared as a rabbit." He even showed up at one of Patterson's workouts with lettuce and carrots. The fight turned ugly, as Ali took offense at Patterson's criticism of his Muslim religion and his name change. When Patterson called him Cassius Clay instead of Muhammad Ali, Ali vowed to punish his opponent. On November 22, 1965, Ali indeed punished Patterson until the referee stopped the bout in the twelfth round. Ali also defeated Patterson a second time in September 1972.

5. THE OCTOPUS

Ali called Ernie Terrell "The Octopus" because of his long arms and sprawling, clutching style. Standing 6'6", Terrell did possess a three-inch reach advantage over Ali, and many experts believed he might pose a tough challenge for the champion. But in February 1967, Ali dominated the taller Terrell and won an unanimous fifteen-round decision. Ali's fight with Terrell followed a similar pattern to his fight with Patterson, because Ali punished both men in the ring for calling him Clay instead of Ali.

6. THE ACORN

Ali tagged Earnie Shavers as "The Acorn" because of his "shiny, bald head." "I'm going into the Garden to pick acorns," Ali said, referring to the fight's location at Madison Square Garden. In addition to a bald head, Shavers possessed a murderous right hand that kay-oed former world champions Jimmy Ellis and Ken Norton in one round. In 1977, Ali captured a close but unanimous decision, surviving a murderous Shavers right hand in the second round.

7. THE PEANUT

In 1980, heavyweight champion Larry Holmes defended his title against Ali, the man who used to hire him as a sparring partner in the 1970s. Ali called Holmes "The Peanut," saying that his head was shaped like a peanut. "I'm going to shell him and send him to Plains, Georgia," Ali said, referring to the hometown of President Jimmy Carter, a former peanut farmer. By the time Ali and Holmes met in the ring, however, Ali's mouth was far more powerful than his fists. Holmes was nearing his prime and Ali was way past his. Holmes dominated the affair, finally winning in the eleventh round.

8. THE PUSSYCAT

In February 1976, Ali defended his title against the limited Belgian Jean-Pierre Coopman. Ali often tried to antagonize his opponents, but Coopman was so respectful of Ali that the champion found it hard to build up any dislike for his overmatched opponent. Coopman would run to kiss Ali when he saw him at prefight press conferences. The promoters called Coopman "The Lion of Flanders," referring to the lion on the Belgian flag. Ali replied: "He's not a lion, he's a pussycat. That's what we'll call him, The Pussycat." When a reporter responded that Coopman's nickname was The Lion, Ali simply purred "meow, meow." Coopman proved to be more like a pussycat than a lion in the ring, as Ali won easily.

9. THE WASHER WOMAN

In March 1966, Ali defended his title against rugged Canadian contender George Chuvalo in Toronto. Ali won a fifteen-round decision, proving much too fast for his slow-footed opponent. Before the bout, Ali dubbed Chuvalo the "Washer Woman." Chuvalo explains Ali's choice of nickname in an interview with the Cyber Boxing Zone: "It was because in the fight with Dejohn, I had his back draped way over the ropes and I already had him knocked out. I had him pinned against the ropes and I started pummeling him, just beating on a knocked-out guy. It looked like I was working on a scrub board. That's why he called me the 'Washer Woman.'" Ali defeated Chuvalo a second time in 1972.

10. DRACULA

Ali dubbed the young Leon Spinks "Dracula" because the young challenger had two front teeth missing. The teeth were lost from blows in previous bouts and, unfortunately, made Spinks an easy target for comedians and critics. But in their first meeting in February 1978, Spinks took a bite out of Ali, upsetting the champion in his eighth pro bout to win the world title by fifteen-round split decision. Ali regained the title later that year, winning a fifteen-round unanimous decision.

Famous Boxing Quotes

The sport of boxing has proven fertile ground for writers, historians, and cinematographers. It also has provided many quotes that have transcended the sport of boxing. The following is a list of ten top quotes or phrases that have become part of American culture or even folklore.

1. **"THE BIGGER THEY ARE, THE HARDER THEY FALL"**

Boxing historians attribute this aphorism to Bob "Ruby Robert" Fitzsimmons, who captured the world heavyweight championship even though he weighed less than 170 pounds. Some claim Fitzsimmons made the comment after he defeated 183-pound "Gentleman" Jim Corbett to win the title on March 17, 1897. Other sources indicate that a thirty-seven-year-old "Ruby Robert" made the comment before facing challenger James J. Jeffries, who weighed more than two hundred pounds his entire career. The much larger and younger Jeffries proved too much for Fitzsimmons and knocked him out. Fitzsimmons certainly made a habit out of beating larger men and captured the middleweight, light heavyweight, and heavyweight titles in his illustrious career. Until Roy Jones defeated John Ruiz to win a heavyweight belt in March 2003, Fitzsimmons was the only former middleweight champion to win the heavyweight crown. Famous author and screenwriter Bud Schulberg borrowed the phrase for his second novel entitled *The Harder They Fall* (1947), which was later made into a movie starring Humphrey Bogart.

2. "HE CAN RUN BUT HE CAN'T HIDE"

Joe Louis, "The Brown Bomber," made this oft-quoted statement before his long-awaited rematch with former light heavyweight king Billy Conn, "The Pittsburgh Kid." In their first meeting in June 1941, Conn outboxed Louis through twelve rounds before an ill-fated attempt in the thirteenth round to trade punches with the heavyweight champion. Conn's change in tactics enabled Louis to land his patented right-hand bomb, dropping Conn for the ten count. The rematch was delayed on more than one occasion by Conn's team for various reasons, including family issues and a broken hand. World War II then delayed the rematch until June 1946. When the rematch finally took place in June 1946, Louis proved true to his word: Conn could not hide from Louis's power punches, and Louis stopped him in the eighth round.

3. "WE WUZ ROBBED"

Joe Jacobs, the manager of heavyweight champion Max Schmeling, uttered this legendary lament to reporters after his fighter dropped a controversial split decision in a rematch with Jack Sharkey on June 21, 1932, to lose the title in Long Island, New York. "They stole the fight from us," Jacobs said. According to many ringside observers, Schmeling had done more than enough to win the fight, but Sharkey got the decision. Even New York mayor Jimmy Walker allegedly told Schmeling that it was a "bum decision." Ironically, the first fight between Schmeling and Sharkey also ended in controversy. In that bout, Sharkey won the first three rounds but lost the fight in the fourth round after landing a low blow that floored Schmeling. Jacobs's classic statement has passed down through the ages with many fighters and managers quoting it when they disagree with a decision.

4. "I CAN LICK ANY SON OF A BITCH IN THE HOUSE"

The legendary John L. Sullivan, the last bare knuckle heavyweight champion, uttered these words, often after drinking a bit too much in Boston bars. More often than not, "The Boston Strong Boy" backed up those words with a terrific punch and tremendous stamina. In 1899, Sullivan defeated Jake Kilrain in the last significant bare knuckle bout after Kilrain could not come out for the seventy-sixth round. Sullivan lost the heavyweight championship to "Gentleman" Jim Corbett in New Orleans in 1892. Both fighters wore five-ounce gloves for the bout. Nearly a century later, "Iron" Mike Tyson would utter a modern-day version of Sullivan's boast when he said: "I'm the baddest man on the planet."

5. "FLOAT LIKE A BUTTERFLY, STING LIKE A BEE"

Cheerleading cornerman Drew "Bundini" Brown coined this saying when speaking about the great Muhammad Ali. Brown and Ali had an unusually strong rapport, and Ali seemed to derive strength from the constant exhortations of Brown. The saying became the mantra of Ali, a heavyweight with a never-before-seen combination of speed and power. Ali himself used the saying before his showdown with George Foreman in Zaire: "Float like a butterfly, sting like a bee. His hands can't hit what his eyes can't see." Ali uttered other memorable boasts, including "I am the greatest" and "I shook up the world," referring to his upset over Sonny Liston to win the heavyweight championship for the first time in 1964.

6. "I AIN'T GOT NO QUARREL WITH THOSE VIET CONG"

Muhammad Ali uttered this famous response to explain his refusal to accept induction into the United States Army. He later expanded his response into one of his patented rhymes: "Keep asking me no matter how long / On the war in Vietnam I sing this song / I ain't got no quarrel with the Viet Cong." Ali's failure to submit to the draft cost him dearly, including a federal indictment (later overturned by the U.S. Supreme Court in June 1971) and the loss of his heavyweight championship at the peak of his career. During his exile from boxing, Ali toured the country, giving speeches at various colleges and universities.

7. "HONEY, I FORGOT TO DUCK"

Heavyweight champion Jack Dempsey uttered this famous response when his wife, actress Estelle Taylor, asked him why he lost his title to Gene Tunney in their September 1926 bout. Dempsey certainly did not avoid many of Tunney's punches during the bout. Tunney's punches closed Dempsey's left eye and left his whole face swollen at the end of the bout. President Ronald Reagan borrowed Dempsey's refrain when speaking to his wife, First Lady Nancy Reagan, as he was recovering from a gunshot wound inflicted by would-be assassin John Hinckley in 1981.

8. "ONLY IN AMERICA"

"Only in America" is the mantra of the illustrious and infamous promoter Don King, who rose from a four-and-a-half-year stint in prison to become boxing's leading promoter. "Only in America can a Don King happen," King has been known to say. "America is the greatest country in the world—I love America." Whatever else one says of King, he is the living embodiment of a rags-to-riches story, going from a numbers runner to inmate to top promoter. He promoted "The Rumble in the Jungle" between Muhammad Ali and George Foreman, "The Thrilla in Manila" between Ali and Joe Frazier, and the "Brawl in Montreal" between Sugar Ray Leonard and Roberto Duran. Muckraking journalist Jack Newfield used King's catchphrase for his 1995 book *Only in America: The Life and Crimes of Don King*. The book was later made into a 1997 HBO hit movie, *Don King: Only in America*.

9. "LET'S GET IT ON"

Former world-class referee Mills Lane first belted out these words during prefight introductions to heavyweight champion Larry Holmes and contender Gerry Cooney during their June 1982 clash for the title. It became Lane's standard phrase that he would say to the fighters before every bout. The phrase became so popular that Lane trademarked it in 1998. He retired from refereeing and formed Let's Get It On Promotions with Tony Holden. They promoted several successful fight cards that were televised by ESPN.

10. **"LET'S GET READY TO RUMBLE"**

Every boxing fan knows ring announcer Michael Buffer's trademarked phrase, which has made him a millionaire. Buffer first belted out his famous five words in 1983 at the Resorts International Hotel in Atlantic City, New Jersey. The rest, as they say, is history. Buffer has parlayed his famous phrase into television appearances and a video game called "Ready to Rumble." His brother, Bruce, runs a company that manages Michael's career. He keeps a powerful law firm on retainer to make sure that people do not violate his trademark rights.

Boxers' Real names

Many professional boxers, including some of the greatest of all time, have changed their names when embarking upon their ring careers. Sometimes the fighter converts to a different religion. Perhaps the best-known example of this is Cassius Marcellus Clay adopting the Muslim name of Muhammad Ali. Other fighters change their names to satisfy the desires of a promoter who wants to appeal to the fight crowd. Other boxers have changed their names in order to reflect their own opinions of themselves. For instance, middleweight great Marvin Hagler added the adjective "Marvelous" to his name, officially becoming Marvelous Marvin Hagler. The following list contains fighters who changed their names for a variety of reasons.

1. **SUGAR RAY ROBINSON**

Born Walker Smith Jr. on May 5, 1921, in Detroit, Michigan, Robinson tagged along to the fights one night with a friend after promising his mother he would not participate in the action. Upon reaching the arena that night, Robinson got word that a flyweight was needed to fill out the card. Smith didn't have the proper registration to compete, but the promoter had a valid card of a retired amateur boxer named Ray Robinson. Smith borrowed the card and the name and went on to become arguably the greatest of all time.

2. JERSEY JOE WALCOTT

Born Arnold Raymond Cream, Jersey Joe Walcott took the name of his boxing hero, the original Joe Walcott, who was a former welterweight champion from Barbados—the country where Cream's father was born. In 1951, Jersey Joe, thirty-seven, became the oldest boxer up to then to win a world heavyweight title. He went on to referee several major bouts and became chairman of the New Jersey Athletic Commission.

3. ARCHIE MOORE

Archie Moore was born Archibald Lee Wright in Benoit, Mississippi, in either 1913 or 1916. His parents divorced at an early age, and young Archie was relocated to St. Louis to live with his uncle Cleveland Moore and aunt Willie Pearl Moore. They changed his last name to Moore.

4. HENRY ARMSTRONG

The only boxer to ever hold three world titles in separate weight classes simultaneously, Armstrong was born Henry Jackson in 1912. At the St. Louis Pine Street YMCA, he met Harry Armstrong, a former boxer, who became his mentor and friend. Armstrong eventually adopted his mentor's last name. Armstrong originally started his career under the name of Melody Jackson, splitting two bouts. But after relocating to California, he resumed his career as Henry Armstrong.

5. ROCKY MARCIANO

Born Rocco Francis Marchegiano, the only man to retire as undefeated heavyweight champion turned pro on March 17, 1947, in Holyoke, Massachusetts, to little fanfare against local amateur Lee Epperson. Marciano fought under the name "Rocky Mack" in his debut because the name sounded Irish and the bout took place on St. Patrick's Day. Rocky's debut didn't appear on his boxing record for several years. Later Rocky would shorten his last name to Marciano in part to assist the Providence, Rhode Island, ring announcer who would regularly bungle the pronunciation.

6. EARNIE SHAVERS

Born Earnie Dee Shaver in 1945 in Garland, Alabama, Earnie's last name was misspelled "Shavers" by local sportswriters when he competed in amateurs. The affable Earnie never bothered to correct them and the name stuck. Years later, Shavers claimed that the improper spelling of his first name on a legal contract with Don King (the contract read "Ernie Shavers") invalidated the contract, and a judge agreed with him.

7. KID CHOCOLATE

Known as "The Cuban Bon Bon," Chocolate was born 1910 in Cuba as Sergio Eligio Sardinas Montalvo and became the first Cuban-born world champ. He claimed both the featherweight and junior lightweight crowns in his ten-year career that spanned from 1928 to 1938. Part of Chocolate's allure was his ability to entertain. The charismatic champion fought with flair and rhythm that was considered decades ahead of its time.

8. KID GAVILAN

Another great Cuban export was Kid Gavilan, born Gerardo Gonzalez in 1926. Gavilan, who held the world welterweight title from 1951 to 1954, was a consummate showman who popularized the "bolo punch," a looping, whirling uppercut that was more flashy than effective. Also known as "The Cuban Hawk," Gavilan twice fought Sugar Ray Robinson and defeated Ike Williams, Beau Jack, and Billy Graham in his 143-bout pro career.

9. TOMMY BURNS

Canada's first heavyweight champion, Burns was born Noah Brusso in Chesley, Ontario, in 1881. Tommy left school at age ten and entered the workforce. At age nineteen, he became a prizefighter in the United States using his birth name. Because Burns's mother strongly objected to her son boxing, he took the Irish-sounding name of Tommy Burns in an attempt to hide his boxing career from her.

10. KHAOSAI GALAXY

Born in 1959 in Thailand as Khaosai Wanghompu, Galaxy turned professional in 1980 in Bangkok. He was a hard-hitting southpaw who made nineteen defenses of his title, only three of which lasted the distance. The former WBA junior bantamweight champion took his last name in honor of his sponsor, a famous nightclub in Bangkok. Galaxy is a hero in Thailand and made six-figure purses that were unmatched until recently. Most Thai fighters take the name of the gym that sponsors their professional career. Galaxy retired with his title intact and a record of 50–1 in 1991.

Here's Your "Sugar" Fix

Famous writer A. J. Liebling called boxing the "Sweet Science." In the hands of a stylish boxer like Willie Pep or the great Ray Robinson, boxing does look sweet. When a boxer possesses quick hands or a pleasing style, sometimes he deservedly receives the moniker "Sugar." The first and best to receive this name was Sugar Ray Robinson, most experts' choice as the greatest pound-for-pound boxer in history.

But other boxers have come along who deserve the honor of having "Sugar" as their nickname, too. Ray Charles Leonard, the darling of the 1976 Montreal Olympics, comes to mind. Other fighters have adopted the nickname as well. The following is a list of ten fighters with Sugar-like nicknames.

1. SUGAR RAY ROBINSON

The original Sugar Ray, Ray Robinson is considered the greater of the two in boxing history. Writer Dave Anderson wrote in his introduction to *Sugar Ray: The Sugar Ray Robinson Story*: "To all those who remember Sugar Ray Robinson as 'pound for pound the best boxer in history,' there has been only one Sugar Ray." He also led the way in terms of style out of the ring. Robinson drove a flamingo-pink Cadillac and was a talented dancer and singer who once pursued a career in the entertainment industry. The former welterweight and middleweight great will always be remembered as the original "Sugar Ray."

2. "SUGAR" RAY LEONARD

"Sugar" Ray Leonard captured the hearts of the American public with his flashy style and electric smile on his way to winning a gold medal at the 1976 Games in Montreal. Leonard reeled off twenty-seven straight victories, capturing the WBA welterweight title from Wilfred Benitez in 1979 via fifteenth-round stoppage. Leonard became the successor to Muhammad Ali as boxing's ambassador to the world. Sugar Ray will be remembered as an all-time great, and his thrilling victories over Thomas Hearns, Roberto Duran, and Marvin Hagler ensured his place in the pantheon of boxing legends.

3. ULTIMINO "SUGAR" RAMOS

Ramos was a former Cuban featherweight titlist who in 1960 was forced to flee his country when Communist leader Fidel Castro cracked down on professional boxing on the island. Ramos relocated to Mexico City to continue his career. On March 21, 1963, Ramos knocked out featherweight champion Davey Moore in the eleventh round to claim the title. Unfortunately, Moore passed away due to head injuries sustained in the contest. Ramos defended his title three times before losing the championship to Vicente Saldivar on September 26, 1964. Ramos continued to box for several years before retiring in 1972 with a record of 54–7–4.

4. CARLOS "SUGAR" DELEON

Carlos DeLeon won the cruiserweight title four times in the 1980s. He captured his first on November 25,

1980, defeating Marvin Camel by fifteen-round decision on the undercard of the famous "No Mas" rematch between Sugar Ray Leonard and Roberto Duran. DeLeon finished his career with a record of 52–8–1. Carlos's son is currently a middleweight prospect fighting under the name Carlos "Baby Sugar" DeLeon Jr.

5.   "SUGAR" SHANE MOSLEY

"Sugar" Shane Mosley won his first thirty-five fights, capturing world lightweight and welterweight titles along the way. He was the second boxer to defeat Oscar De La Hoya. Mosley was on his way to a spot among boxing immortals until he met Vernon Forrest and lost two consecutive decisions that have at least temporarily dulled his luster. Mosley has embarked on a comeback in hopes of reclaiming the mythical title of pound-for-pound world's best boxer.

6.   GEORGE "SUGAR" COSTNER

George "Sugar" Costner was a top welterweight contender in the 1940s who defeated Hall of Famers Ike Williams and Kid Gavilan in his career. From Cincinnati, Ohio, Costner never received a world title shot, but he faced many top contenders and champions. Twice he was stopped in the first round by the great Sugar Ray Robinson. Costner retired in 1950 with two detached retinas. Several eye operations could not bring back his eyesight. Blinded, Costner somehow graduated from Cleveland State University and later worked for the Ohio Civil Rights Commission.

7.   "SUGAR" RAY SEALES

"Sugar" Ray Seales was the only American to capture a gold medal at the 1972 Olympic Games in Munich, Germany. Seales campaigned as a middleweight during the late 1970s and early 1980s. He won his first twenty-one fights until losing a close decision to Marvin Hagler in Hagler's backyard of Boston. Later, he fought Hagler to a draw, but then Hagler scored a first-round kayo in their rubber match. Seales finished with a career record of 56–8–3 and fought his final fights nearly blind due to a detached retina.

8. GARNET "SUGAR" HART

Philadelphia's Garnet "Sugar" Hart was a solid top-ten welterweight contender for much of the 1950s and early 1960s. He held wins over fighters such as Clarence Harris, Charley "Tombstone" Smith, and Ralph Dupas. He lost to future world champions Luis "El Feo" Rodriguez and Benny "Kid" Paret. He retired in 1961 with a record of 29–7–2.

9. "SUCRA" RAY OLIVEIRA

"Sucra" is Spanish for "sugar," making Oliveira eligible for this list. Oliveira, a two-time NABF champion, has a sturdy chin that belongs on Mt. Rushmore. The New Bedford, Massachusetts–based welterweight has never been stopped in over fifty contests and is hoping to secure another shot at a world title in the near future. He has been involved in fights that set Compubox records for the number of punches thrown.

10. ANDRE "SUGARMAN" COOPER

Cooper was a 1980s middleweight who received his nickname for a resemblance to Sugar Ray Robinson. Cooper won his first ten bouts before losing a decision to Mike Tinley for the New Jersey State title on September 9, 1984. Cooper lost again the next year by knockout to Lindell Holmes and faded into obscurity.

Just Call Me "Kid"

Many great boxers have been tagged with the nick-name "Kid" as part of their ring personas. The appellation was particularly popular during the early part of the twentieth century when fighters often turned professional at a very young age. Many former champions and Hall of Fame fighters have taken the name "Kid."

1. CHARLES "KID" MCCOY

Born Norman Selby, Charles "Kid" McCoy is one of the most unusual and controversial characters in boxing history. He won the world middleweight title in 1897 but never defended his title. He fought at light heavy-weight and even heavyweight against larger men. McCoy claimed to have invented the "corkscrew" punch, in which he twisted his fist at the point of impact. He was known on occasion to not fight to the best of his ability. After he defeated heavyweight contender Joe Choynski in 1900, a newspaper ran the headline that Choynski was "beaten by the Real McCoy." The phrase stays with us to this day. McCoy was later convicted of manslaughter for killing the woman with whom he lived. Only his dramatic courtroom testimony saved him from the death penalty. After his release from prison, he committed suicide.

2. KID CHOCOLATE

Born in Cuba as Eligio Sardinias-Montalbo, Kid Chocolate, the "Cuban Bon Bon," thrilled fans with his blazing hand speed and power punching. He never lost as an amateur and won his first twenty-one pro bouts by knockout. His flashy ring style earned him many admirers. He won the world junior lightweight title in 1931 and retired in 1938 with a ring record of 131–9–6.

3. TED "KID" LEWIS

Born Gershon Mendeloff in London, England, Terry "Kid" Lewis turned pro at the age of fourteen. He won the world welterweight championship in 1915 with a decision over arch rival Jack Britton. He lost and then regained the title from Britton in 1917. He fought from 1909 until 1929, compiling a record of 173–30–14 with sixty-five no-decisions.

4. DIXIE KID

Born Aaron Lister Brown in Fulton, Missouri, the Dixie Kid fought professionally from 1900 to 1920. He won the world welterweight championship over fellow African-American great Joe Walcott in 1904. He held the title until 1912 when he lost to Harry Lewis. The Dixie Kid was known for his unique style of holding his hands by his side, daring his opponents to strike him. His record was 80–29–12 with nearly thirty no-decisions.

5. JACKIE "KID" BERG

Born Judah Bergman in an area of London called Whitechapel, Jackie "Kid" Berg turned professional in

1924 and won the world junior welterweight championship in 1930. Later that year, he won a ten-round split decision over the then-undefeated Kid Chocolate. Berg's active fight pace also earned him the moniker the "Whitechapel Whirlwind." He fought from 1924 to 1945, earning a record of 157–26–9.

6. GEORGE "KID" LAVIGNE

George "Kid" Lavigne stood only 5'3", but he loomed large in the boxing world during his heyday. He was called the Saginaw Kid because he was from Saginaw, Michigan. He turned pro at age seventeen in 1886 and won the world lightweight championship in 1886. He holds two victories over the great Joe Walcott and retired in 1909 with a record of 35–6–10 with five no-decisions.

7. KID GAVILAN

Cuba's Kid Gavilan, born Gerardo Gonzalez, thrilled fight fans in the 1940s and 1950s with his ring flair and style. He is often credited with popularizing the flashy "bolo punch," a roundhouse, arching uppercut. Turning pro at the age of sixteen in 1943, Kid Gavilan won the world welterweight title in 1951. He fought until 1958, retiring with a record of 107–30–6. He was never knocked out.

8. KID WILLIAMS

Kid Williams, who was born John Gutenko in Denmark, was the world bantamweight champion from 1914 to 1917. He turned pro at the age of sixteen and fought more than two hundred bouts in a career that spanned from 1910 to 1929. He was known for his aggressive, crowd-pleasing style. His record was 104–17–9 with seventy-one no-decisions.

9. ANTONIO "KID PAMBELE" CERVANTES

Antonio "Kid Pambele" Cervantes was a master boxer who twice held the WBA junior welterweight championship, from 1972 to 1976 and 1977 to 1980. He lost his crown to two fellow Hall of Famers—Wilfred Benitez in 1976 and Aaron Pryor in 1980. He was the first Colombian to ever win a world title. His uncle nicknamed him "Kid Pambele." The word "Pambele" means "strong." He retired in 1983 with a record of 66–12–1.

10. BENNY "KID" PARET

Benny "Kid" Paret was a Cuban boxer who won the world welterweight title twice. He first won the title in 1959 with a victory over Don Jordan. He lost and regained the title in two bouts with Emile Griffith. In 1962, Griffith won the tragic rubber match when he battered Paret unconscious as the Cuban lay slumped in a corner. The twenty-five-year-old Paret died during surgery on his brain after the bout. His record was 36–12–1.

nonagenarians

Boxing can be a brutal, stressful existence for just about everybody connected with the business. But some fighters and others associated closely with boxing managed to live until their nineties, making them nonagenarians. A few on the list, including Max Schmeling and Jimmy McLarnin, are still living at the time of this writing.

1. MAX SCHMELING

Max Schmeling is the oldest living fighter in the world. He is, at the time of this writing, ninety-seven years old. Schmeling won the world heavyweight title in 1930 with a disqualification win over Jack Sharkey. He lost the title to Sharkey two years later. Schmeling is best remembered for his two fights against the great Joe Louis. The German handed Louis his first loss as a pro in 1936 but lost in the first round in their 1938 rematch.

2. JIMMY MCLARNIN

Jimmy "Baby Face" McLarnin won the world welterweight championship twice, in 1933 and in 1934. He fought fifteen world champions in his career, defeating thirteen of them. He defeated such great fighters as Pancho Villa, Benny Leonard, Barney Ross, and Lou Ambers. He retired at the age of twenty-nine while still at the top of his game. Born in Dublin, Ireland, in 1905, McLarnin still is alive, residing in the state of Washington.

3. JACK SHARKEY

Born Joseph Paul Zukauskas, Jack Sharkey won the world heavyweight championship in 1932 with a victory over Max Schmeling. He lost the title to Italian giant Primo Carnera. Sharkey also lost bouts to heavyweight greats Jack Dempsey and Joe Louis. He died on August 17, 1994, at the age of ninety-one.

4. JOHNNY WILSON

Johnny Wilson, former middleweight champion of the world, died at the age of ninety-two on December 8, 1985. His real name was John F. Panica. He won the middleweight title in 1920 by defeating Mike O'Dowd. He lost the crown in 1923 to the great Harry Greb. He died in a Massachusetts nursing home.

5. RAY ARCEL

Ray Arcel trained twenty world champions, including such greats as Roberto Duran and Tony Zale. He trained his first world champion, Frankie Genarro, in 1923 and his last, Larry Holmes, in 1982. He died at the age of ninety-four in March 1994. He was inducted into the International Boxing Hall of Fame in 1991.

6. EDDIE FUTCH

The legendary Eddie Futch trained twenty-two world champions up until age eighty-six. Futch began as a boxer, winning the Detroit Golden Gloves as a light-weight in 1933. He did not box professionally after it was discovered he had a heart murmur. He trained Joe Frazier and Ken Norton to victories over Muhammad Ali. Futch died in October 2001 at the age of ninety.

7. GILBERT ODD

England's Gilbert Odd was one of the greatest histori-ans the sport of boxing has ever known. In 1945, he became editor of *Boxing News* and created the *Boxing News Annual and Record Book*. He wrote more than a dozen books, including *Ring Battles of the Century* (1948), *Debatable Decisions* (1953), and *The Encyclo-pedia of Boxing* (1983). He died in 1996 at the age of ninety-three.

8. HARRY MARKSON

Harry Markson was one of the greatest publicists in the history of boxing. He served as publicity director for Mike Jacobs, head of the Twentieth Century Sporting Club. He later held a high position with the International Boxing Club (IBC), which controlled boxing for most of the 1950s. He later became president of Madison Square Garden Boxing, Inc. He died in November 1998 at the age of ninety-two.

9. DON DUNPHY

Don Dunphy, "The Voice of Boxing," called thousands of boxing fights over radio and television during his il-lustrious career. He called fights for Gillette Safety Razor Corporation in the 1940s and 1950s. He later called many fights on closed-circuit, including Ali–Frazier I. He also broadcast New York Yankees games. He died in July 1998 at the age of ninety.

10. **CHRIS DUNDEE**

Chris Dundee was a manager and promoter who promoted many top fights from his home base in Miami Beach, Florida. He started managing fighters in 1928 and guided Ezzard Charles to the world heavyweight title in 1949. For many years, he owned and operated the Fifth Street Gym in Miami Beach. He was the brother of the great trainer Angelo Dundee and Joe Dundee, a former club fighter. He died in November 1998 at the age of ninety-one.

Female Firsts

Boxing is no longer an all-male sport. Pushed to the fringes and even prohibited for years, women's boxing has made substantial progress in the past decade. Now, many professional fight cards feature female bouts. The emergence of Christy Martin and Laila Ali, the daughter of Muhammad Ali, as potential superstars has taken female boxing to even higher levels.

1. AILEEN EATON

Aileen Eaton became the first and only distaff member of the International Boxing Hall of Fame when she was inducted in 2002. Eaton and her husband, Cal, promoted weekly boxing shows at Los Angeles' Olympic Auditorium for nearly forty years. She promoted a championship triple-header in 1963 featuring Sugar Ramos–Davey Moore, Emile Griffith–Luis Rodriguez, and Battling Torres–Roberto Cruz.

2. CHRISTY MARTIN

In 1996, Christy Martin, known as the "The Coal Miner's Daughter," fought Diedre Gogarty on the undercard of a Mike Tyson–Frank Bruno heavyweight championship fight. It was the first female fight shown on a pay-per-view telecast. The battle was seen by an estimated 1.1 million viewers and instantly made women's boxing and Martin more popular. The slugger with a potent left hook has a record of 45–3–2 with thirty-one kayoes.

3. LADY TYGER TRIMIAR

This female boxing star of the 1970s and 1980s achieved fame for going on a month-long hunger strike in 1987 to protest to promoters' failure to promote women's boxing. She picketed Don King's Manhattan office. She also sued the state of New York to obtain a boxing license. She fought from 1973 to 1987. She captured the world lightweight title in 1979 by defeating Sue Carlson.

4. EVA SHAIN

Eva Shain became the first woman to judge a world title bout when in 1977 she was one of the judges for Muhammad Ali's defense against Earnie Shavers. She got her license in 1975 and judged more than five thousand fights. She was married to ring announcer Frank Shain.

5. BARBARA BUTTRICK

In 1954, Barbara Buttrick of Yorkshire, England, became the first female boxer to have a fight broadcast on national television. Because England would not allow professional matches between females, Buttrick and her husband moved to the United States in 1952. In 1957, she defeated Phyllis Kugler in San Antonio, Texas, to win a world title. Her career record was 30–1–1, with twelve kayoes.

6. JENNIFER MCLEERY

Bellingham, Washington, teenager Jennifer McLeery, who used the name Dallas Malloy, sued USA Boxing in 1991 for the right to participate as an amateur boxer. In October 1993, USA Boxing's board of governors allowed female boxing after a judge ruled in favor of Malloy. Malloy won a decision over Heather Poyner in the first female bout officially sanctioned by USA Boxing.

7. MARGARET MCGREGOR

Margaret McGregor achieved notoriety when she defeated male boxer Loi Chow of Vancouver, Canada, on October 9, 1999. Washington state officials approved the mixed-gender bout. However, the Association of Boxing Commissions would not recognize the bout, calling it an exhibition. McGregor, who was a kickboxer before turning pro, won a unanimous four-round decision.

8. JACKIE KALLEN

Called the "First Lady of Boxing," Jackie Kallen parlayed experience as a sportswriter and publicist for Thomas Hearns into a career as a manager. Her claim to fame was managing former middleweight and super middleweight champion James "Lights Out" Toney. She later wrote a book entitled *Hit Me with Your Best Shot: A Fight Plan for Dealing with All of Life's Hard Knocks.* Her story will soon come to the big screen in *Against the Ropes: The Jackie Kallen Story.*

9. BELLA BURGE

Bella Burge was boxing's first significant female promoter. She began in the business of promoting fights with her husband, Dick, a former British lightweight champion. From 1915 until 1940, she promoted hundreds of fights in London, England.

10. **BELLE MARTEL**

In 1940, Belle Martel of Van Nuys, California, became the first female boxing referee when she officiated eight bouts in San Bernardino, California. There are still very few female referees. Unfortunately, gender discrimination forced Martel to end her refereeing career shortly after it began. The California Athletic Commission adopted new rules prohibiting women referees. According to a 1940 *New York Times* article, Martel responded: "The stupid and ridiculous charges stirred up during the past month [since her refereeing pro bouts] have brought about my decision to step out and give the men, who have been blasting so loudly, a chance to see what they can do for boxing."

Black Pioneers

Sadly, the sport of boxing has experienced its own share of the racial prejudice and bias that has plagued American society since its inception. Peter Jackson and other top black boxers were denied a chance to win a world title because of their skin color. Even fighters in the lighter weight divisions, such as George Dixon and Joe Gans, who were given world title shots had to accept smaller purses than they deserved. Each of these great champions died penniless after their great careers. The situation improved somewhat in the 1930s after Joe Louis became the second African-American to win the heavyweight title. Louis was, in the immortal words of sportswriter Jimmy Cannon, "a credit to his race—the human race."

The following is a list of early African-American or black (some in the list were not Americans) fighters who can truly be considered pioneers.

1. BILL RICHMOND

Bill Richmond, known as the "Black Terror," was probably the first black man to achieve fame in the sport of boxing. Born a slave in Richmond, New York, Richmond came under the command of British general Earl Percy. Richmond distinguished himself in sparring with British soldiers. Percy took Richmond back to England as his valet. Richmond won several bouts before he challenged the great Tom Cribb for the English heavyweight title. Though he was much older and lighter, he gave Cribb a good battle before succumbing in the twenty-fifth round. Richmond later served as trainer for Tom Molineaux.

2. TOM MOLINEAUX

Born a Virginia slave in 1784, Tom Molineaux earned his freedom from owner Algernon Molineaux by winning a bout against the slave of another plantation owner. Molineaux then traveled to England to pursue fame in boxing. In December 1810, he fought legendary champion Tom Cribb. In the twenty-eighth round, Molineaux floored Cribb for more than thirty seconds. He should have been declared the champion, but Cribb's supporters claimed foul, and the referee allowed the bout to continue. Cribb won in the thirty-third round. Molineaux lost badly in the rematch as his training habits had declined. He died in Ireland at the age of thirty-four.

3. GEORGE DIXON

The Canadian-born George Dixon, known as "Little Chocolate," became the first black man to win a world boxing championship when he captured the bantamweight championship from Nunc Wallace in London, England, in 1890. He later added the world featherweight title when he defeated Fred Johnson in Cooney Island in 1892. His 1892 defeat of Jack Skelly, a white fighter, in New Orleans, led to a near race riot. Dixon fought until 1906 and died in 1909.

4. JACK JOHNSON

Jack Johnson became the first African-American heavyweight champion of the world when he kayoed champion Tommy Burns in their 1908 encounter in Australia. Johnson had to pursue Burns halfway across the globe before landing a title shot. Born in Galveston, Texas, Johnson traveled far and wide to gain greater boxing experience. White America reacted with collective agony to Johnson's championship reign. Many cried out for a "Great White Hope" to come rescue the title. Johnson repelled all challengers, including previously unbeaten former champion Jim Jeffries, until losing to Jess Willard in Cuba under circumstances some consider rather dubious in 1915. There has been speculation that perhaps Johnson threw the fight in exchange for authorities in the United States dropping federal charges against him. Others believe that years of inadequate training finally caught up with Johnson when he faced a younger, larger man in Willard.

5. JOE GANS

Born Joseph Gaines in Baltimore, Maryland, Joe Gans became the first native-born African-American to win a world title. In 1902, he kayoed Frank Erne in Fort Erie, Ontario, for the lightweight crown. Gans studied Erne's style diligently after losing to Erne in his first attempt at the title in 1900. He battled the great Joe Walcott to a draw in 1904 for the welterweight title. He finally lost the lightweight crown in 1908 to Battling Nelson and retired the next year. Only one year after retirement, he died—gone but not forgotten.

6. JOE WALCOTT

Joe Walcott was called the "Barbados Demon" because he was born in Barbados, British West Indies. Though standing less than 5'2", he was a giant in the ring. He lost in his first two world title attempts for the lightweight and welterweight titles against George "Kid" Lavigne and Mysterious Billy Smith in 1897 and 1898, respectively. But in 1901 he stopped Jim "Rube" Ferns to win the welterweight crown. In 1904, he lost the title on a foul to the Dixie Kid in the first world title bout between two African-American fighters. Walcott retired in 1911.

7. PETER JACKSON

Peter Jackson was a remarkable fighter and human being who was denied a shot at the world heavyweight championship because of the color line. Born in 1861 in St. Croix, West Indies, he and his family traveled to Australia. Jackson won the Australian heavyweight title in 1886. In 1891, he battled future world heavyweight champion James Corbett to a sixty-one-round draw. Corbett later stated Jackson was the best fighter he had ever fought. Jackson acted in plays and ran a boxing school in London. He retired in 1899. His grave in Toowang Cemetery in Australia appropriately reads: "This was a man."

8. JOHN HENRY LEWIS

Born in 1914, John Henry Lewis became the first African-American to win the world light heavyweight crown when he defeated Bob Olin in 1935. A relative of the great Tom Molineaux, Lewis turned pro as a welterweight in 1928 at the age of fourteen. He held his light heavyweight crown for four years. He abdicated the crown when Joe Louis gave him a shot at the world heavyweight title. Unfortunately, Lewis was no match for the younger and stronger Louis, losing in the first round. Lewis retired after the loss.

9. JACK BLACKBURN

Born in 1883, Jack Blackburn was a top lightweight in the early twentieth century who earned greater acclaim as the trainer of the legendary Joe Louis, the heavyweight champion of the world. Blackburn fought great fighters such as Joe Gans, Sam Langford, and Philadelphia Jack O'Brien. His career was put on hold in 1909 after he shot three people, including his wife. Sentenced to ten to fifteen years in prison, he was released for good behavior after serving nearly five years. Blackburn resumed boxing after his release and then became a trainer. He trained Sammy Mandell to the lightweight crown and Bud Taylor to the bantamweight title. But his greatest pupil was the great Joe Louis, who affectionately called him "Chappie." With managers John Roxborough and Julian Black, Blackburn formed an all-African-American team that closely counseled Louis on how to win and how to behave during his heavyweight reign.

10. ZACK CLAYTON

Zack Clayton became the first African-American to referee a world heavyweight title fight when in 1952 he refereed the third bout between Ezzard Charles and Jersey Joe Walcott. He also refereed the famous Ali–Foreman "Rumble in the Jungle" in Kinshasa, Zaire, in 1974. Clayton was a fine athlete in his own right, playing baseball in the Negro leagues for twelve years and also playing basketball for the Harlem Globetrotters.

Puerto Rican Greats

The beautiful island of Puerto Rico, located about one thousand miles southeast of Florida, is a commonwealth of the United States, but it remains independent in spirit and proud of its rich heritage. This island has also been home to many great boxers. The following are ten of the greatest fighters from Puerto Rico.

1. SIXTO ESCOBAR

The diminutive Escobar only stood 5'4" but became a giant in Puerto Rican boxing history as the island's first world champion. He captured the NBA bantamweight title in 1934 with a kayo over Baby Casanova and the world bantamweight championship in 1936 with a stoppage of Tony Marino. He possessed a powerful right hand and a granite chin that kept him upright in seventy-two professional bouts. He was elected to the International Boxing Hall of Fame and had a stadium named after him in Puerto Rico's capital city of San Juan.

2. **CARLOS ORTIZ**

Born in Puerto Rico, Ortiz moved with his family to New York when he was a kid. He turned pro at the age of eighteen and won his first twenty bouts. In 1959, he won the world junior welterweight crown. In 1962, he won the more highly regarded world lightweight title with a victory over fellow Hall of Famer Joe Brown. Ortiz lost and regained his title in fights with Panama's great Ismael Laguna. He also defended his title against such greats as Ultiminio "Sugar" Ramos and Flash Elorde. He retired in 1972 with a record of 61–7–1.

3. **JOSE TORRES**

Jose Torres was a great, light heavyweight champion who lost only three bouts of forty-five fights in his professional career. Born in Puerto Rico, he joined the U.S. Army after some trouble in his youth. He represented the United States in the 1956 Melbourne Olympics, winning a silver medal in the middleweight division. In the finals, he dropped a narrow 3–2 decision to fellow Hall of Famer Lazlo Papp of Hungary. Torres won the world light heavyweight championship from Willie Pastrano in 1965 and defended his title three times until losing by decision to Dick Tiger. Torres has accomplished much outside of the boxing ring for his favorite sport, serving as New York State athletic chairman and president of the World Boxing Organization, as well as authoring books on Muhammad Ali and Mike Tyson.

4. **WILFREDO GOMEZ**

Known as "Bazooka," Wilfredo Gomez won world titles in three different weight classes—junior featherweight,

featherweight, and junior lightweight. In 1977, he won his first title at junior featherweight and proceeded to dominate the division by defending his title seventeen times. In 1984, he decisioned Juan LaPorte to win the featherweight crown, and a year later outpointed Rocky Lockridge to win the junior lightweight title. He did lose probably the biggest fight of his career, a 1981 showdown with Mexican great Salvador Sanchez, billed as the "Battle of the Little Giants." Sanchez stopped him in the eighth round. Gomez retired in 1989 with a record of 44–3–1.

5. WILFRED BENITEZ

Wilfred Benitez was truly a boxing prodigy and one of the finest ring technicians of his era. He captured the world junior welterweight championship at the age of seventeen with a narrow decision win over the legendary Antonio "Kid Pambele" Cervantes. He added the welterweight crown in 1979 by outpointing Carlos Palomino. A crushing one-punch knockout of Maurice Hope in 1981 gave Benitez his third world title in the junior middleweight division. In his prime, the self-proclaimed "Bible of Boxing" would show off his remarkable defensive skills by evading punches on the ropes. Sadly, Benitez's skills declined in later years, and he became a shadow of his former self.

6. FELIX TRINIDAD

Felix "Tito" Trinidad possessed a fearsome left hook, quick hands, and a killer instinct that led him to glory in the welterweight, junior middleweight, and, briefly, the middleweight divisions. For most of his career he campaigned at welterweight, winning the IBF crown in 1993 and holding it through a 1999 victory over Oscar

De La Hoya. Trinidad then moved up to junior middle-weight and dominated former gold medalist David Reid. He added a middleweight title in 2001 with a crushing kayo over William Joppy. The only loss in his career came in his penultimate bout against middle-weight great Bernard Hopkins, who stopped him in the twelfth round. Until his loss to Hopkins, Tito was considered, along with Roy Jones Jr., as the best pound-for-pound fighter in the world.

7. **ESTEBAN DEJESUS**

Esteban DeJesus will forever be best known as the chief rival of and first man to defeat the legendary Roberto Duran. The two rivals fought three bouts at light-weight, with DeJesus winning the first and Duran taking the last two. In each of the first two bouts, DeJesus dropped Duran with his patented punch—a devastating left hook. He won the WBC world lightweight title in 1976 and defended it three times before a unification bout with Duran. He retired in 1980 after losing to Saoul Mamby for the WBC junior welterweight crown with a record of 57–5. DeJesus died of AIDS in prison while serving a life sentence for murder.

8. **HECTOR CAMACHO**

Hector "Macho" Camacho may be known today mostly for his flashy and at times outrageous personality. But at his best Camacho used blazing hand and foot speed to fight his way to the top of the boxing world. He never really lost in his prime, winning world titles at super featherweight and lightweight by defeating the likes of Rafael "Bazooka" Limon, Jose Luis Ramirez, and fellow Puerto Rican great Edwin Rosario. When past his prime, he lost decisions to Felix Trinidad, Julio Cesar

Chavez, and Oscar De La Hoya in world title matches. Still active, his record at the end of 2002 was 75–4–2. His son, Hector Camacho Jr., is a junior welterweight contender.

٩. EDWIN ROSARIO

The talented Edwin "Chapo" Rosario was a three-time world lightweight champion and one-time world junior welterweight champion who could seemingly beat any foe but drugs. A master boxer with power, Rosario decisioned rival Jose Luis Ramirez in 1983 for his first world title. Three years later, he crushed Livingstone Bramble in the second round to win a second title. Three years after that, he kayoed Anthony Jones for his third lightweight crown. While still an active boxer, Rosario died in 1997 of acute pulmonary edema,

Bob Lynch

Puerto Rican flyweight great Eric Morel, wearing his flag on his trunks, prepares to unload his right hand.

thought to be aggravated by a long history of drug abuse. His record was 47–6.

10. **ERIC MOREL**

Born and raised in Puerto Rico, Morel relocated to Madison, Wisconsin, in time for his freshman year in high school. Morel represented the United States as an Olympian in 1996, losing a decision to the eventual gold medal winner, Cuba's Maikro Romero. Known as "Little Hands of Steel" for his quick and strong punching ability, Morel captured the WBA flyweight title with a twelve-round decision over Sornpichai Kratingdaenggym in his hometown in August 2000. Morel has won thirty-three straight professional bouts and defended his throne five times. In the ring, Morel proudly displays the flag and colors of his native homeland.

Colombian Champions

The country of Colombia in northern South America has produced a host of world champions. Antonio "Kid Pambele" Cervantes became the country's first champion in 1972. Since then many of his compatriots have followed suit. The following are ten world champions from Colombia.

1. ANTONIO CERVANTES

Antonio "Kid Pambele" Cervantes became Colombia's first world champion when he stopped Alfonzo Frazier in the tenth round in 1972 to capture the WBA junior welterweight belt. He made ten successful title defenses until a split-decision loss to the Puerto Rican prodigy Wilfred Benitez. After Benitez failed to give him a rematch, the WBA stripped Benitez. In June 1977, Cervantes stopped Carlos Gimenez to win the vacant WBA title. In his second reign as champion, Cervantes made six successful title defenses before Aaron Pryor stopped him in August 1980.

2. RODRIGO VALDEZ

Rodrigo "Rocky" Valdez, Colombia's second world champion, twice won the world middleweight title. In

1974, he stopped the tough Bennie Briscoe to win the WBC belt. He made four successful defenses until he lost a fifteen-round unanimous decision to WBA champion Carlos Monzon in a title unification match. He also lost another decision to Monzon in a rematch. After Monzon retired, Valdez again defeated Briscoe, this time by decision, to win the WBC and WBA belts in 1977. He lost in his first title defense to Hugo Corro.

3. RICARDO CARDONA

Ricardo Cardona won the WBA world super bantamweight title in May 1978 with a twelfth-round stoppage of Korean Soo-Hwan Hong. He made five successful defenses until he faced former Olympic gold medalist Leo Randolph in May 1980. Randolph became the first member of the vaunted 1976 United States Olympic team to win a professional world title when he upset Cardona. Cardona would lose in another world title bid in 1981 and never received another title shot, retiring in 1984.

4. PRUDENCIO CARDONA

Prudencio Cardona captured the WBC flyweight world title in March 1982 with a first-round kayo over Antonio Avelar. Cardona lost the title in his first world title defense, dropping a fifteen-round decision to Freddy Castillo in July 1982. He failed in his only other world title shot in 1984 and finally retired in June 1992 after losing thirteen of his last fourteen fights.

5. RUBEN PALACIO

Ruben Palacio won the WBO world featherweight title in his last bout—an eighth-round stoppage of Colin Mc-Millan in September 1992. McMillan was ahead on the scorecards but suffered a dislocated shoulder. Palacio had to retire because it was discovered forty-eight hours before his first scheduled title defense that he was HIV-positive for the AIDS virus. He was not allowed to fight again.

6. LUIS MENDOZA

Luis Mendoza won the WBA world super bantamweight title with a third-round stoppage of countryman Ruben Palacio in September 1990. It was the second title bout between the two compatriots, as their first bout for the vacant title ended in a twelve-round draw. Mendoza successfully defended his title four times before dropping a decision to Raul Perez in October 1991. Mendoza lost in four more world title shots, finally retiring in 1998 after losing to the talented but troubled American Freddie Norwood.

7. JORGE ELICIER JULIO

Jorge Elicier Julio won the WBA world bantamweight title in October 1992 with a decision win over Eddie Cook. He made two successful defenses before losing to unbeaten American Junior Jones in October 1993. In July 1997, he won a twelve-round split decision over Oscar Maldonado to win the WBO world bantamweight crown. He made three successful defenses before losing a decision to the colorful Johnny Tapia in January 2000. Julio lost badly to Manny Pacquaio in a bid for the IBF super bantamweight title in June 2002.

8. HAROLD GREY

Harold Grey is a former two-time world champion in the junior bantamweight division who decisioned Julio Cesar Borboa in 1994 to win the IBF belt. He successfully defended his title three times before a split decision loss to Carlos Salazar in October 1995. He regained the title from Salazar in April 1996 but lost in his first defense to power-punching Danny Romero in August 1996.

9. BEBIS MENDOZA

Bebis Mendoza won the WBA junior flyweight championship in August 2000 when referee Mitch Halpern disqualified Nicaragua's Rosendo Alvarez for repeated low blows. Mendoza lost his title in his first defense in an immediate rematch against Alvarez by split decision in March 2001. By October 2003, his record stood at 29–2 with twenty-four kayoes.

10. IRENE PACHECO

Irene Pacheco won the IBF flyweight title in April 1999 with a ninth-round stoppage of Luis Cox. As of this writing, he has made six successful defenses and stands at 30–0.

Born in Georgia

Over the years many great fighters have come from the Southern state of Georgia. Former cruiser-weight and three-time world heavyweight champion Evander Holyfield has lived most of his life in Atlanta, though he was born in Atmore, Alabama. The following champions and top contenders were all born in the "Peach State."

1. YOUNG STRIBLING

William Lawrence Stribling, better known as Young Stribling, was born in Bainbridge, Georgia, in 1904. He kayoed more than one hundred opponents in a professional boxing career that was tragically cut short by a fatal motorcycle accident at age twenty-eight. He lost in separate fights for the light heavyweight and heavyweight crowns.

2. TIGER FLOWERS

Born in 1895 in Camille, Georgia, Theodore "Tiger" Flowers made his pro debut in Brunswick, Georgia, in 1918. Known as the "Georgia Deacon" because of his devout religious beliefs, he recited a passage from

Psalms before his bouts. Flowers became the first African-American to win the world middleweight title when he defeated the great Harry Greb in 1926.

3. IKE WILLIAMS

Isiah "Ike" Williams was born in Brunswick, Georgia, in 1923, though his family moved to New Jersey in his youth. It was there that he made his professional debut in 1940. He won the National Boxing Association lightweight title in 1945 and universal recognition as 135-pound champion two years later. Today, he is regarded as one of the division's greatest fighters.

4. BEAU JACK

Beau Jack was born Sidney Walker in Augusta, Georgia, in 1921. He worked at the Augusta National Golf Club, which hosts the famous Masters golf tournament, as a teenager. He moved to Massachusetts to pursue a boxing career with money from golfing great Bobby Jones. Jack won the New York World lightweight title in 1942. He fought multiple bouts against fellow Georgia-born great Ike Williams.

5. EZZARD CHARLES

Ezzard Mack Charles was born in 1921 in Lawrenceville, Georgia. He moved to Cincinnati in his youth and started boxing there. He became known as the Cincinnati Cobra by dint of his lethal left jab and fine boxing ability. He dominated the light heavyweight division but never received a title shot at 175 pounds because he was too good for his own good. Charles did win the world heavyweight title in 1949, beating his rival Jersey Joe Walcott. Today, he is perhaps best remembered for two losses to Rocky Marciano.

6. JIMMY BIVINS

Born in Dry Branch, Georgia, in 1919, James Louis Bivins moved to Cleveland, Ohio, with his family when he was only two years old. He made his professional debut in Cleveland in 1940 and fought until 1955, facing many top fighters in his Hall of Fame career. He is one of the greatest fighters never to receive a world title shot, although while then-heavyweight champion Joe Louis served in the U.S. Army during World War II, Bivins was recognized in some circles as "duration champion."

7. LARRY HOLMES

Larry Holmes was born in Cuthbert, Georgia, in 1949. His family moved to Easton, Pennsylvania, when he was six years old. Holmes, who still resides in Easton, became known as the "Easton Assassin." His great left jab carried him to the world heavyweight title in 1978 via a thrilling split-decision win over Ken Norton. Holmes held one or the other version of the world title until 1985, making a remarkable twenty title defenses. Amazingly, Holmes fought in 2002 at the age of fifty-three, winning a ten-round decision over Butterbean.

8. VERNON FORREST

Vernon Forrest was born in Augusta, Georgia, in 1971 and still resides in his home state in the capital city of Atlanta. A 1992 Olympian, he catapulted to boxing prominence in 2002 with two wins over previously unbeaten "Sugar" Shane Mosley. Most boxing authorities pegged Forrest as "Fighter of the Year" for 2002. He lost his world title in early 2003 to hard-punching Nicaraguan warrior Ricardo Mayorga.

9. LLOYD MARSHALL

Lloyd Marshall, known as "Black Dynamite," was born in Madison County, Georgia, in 1914. He turned pro in 1936 and fought many top middleweights and light heavyweights until his retirement in 1951. He never received a world title shot in part due to the color barrier. During his career, he scored victories over great fighters such as Charley Burley and Ezzard Charles.

10. SAM GARR

Sam "Bam Bam" Garr is a current junior middleweight contender who was born in Stone Mountain, Georgia, in 1969. He lost a twelve-round decision in 1999 for the world welterweight crown to James Page. He now campaigns at 154 pounds and seeks another world title shot.

Homegrown Heroes

A common boxing expression is "hometown fighter." Such a fighter often does battle in his own backyard, with hundreds or thousands of fans screaming for his triumph. These boxers frequently have great advantages over their out-of-town opponents, as the hometown fighters may enjoy close ties with the promoter and the crowd.

1. SEAN O'GRADY

Boxing under the tutelage of his father, Pat O'Grady, Sean turned pro at age fifteen in Oklahoma City. O'Grady fought fifty-nine more times in Oklahoma City, winning every fight. The former champion and current boxing broadcaster only lost on the road against contenders. O'Grady won his biggest fight on the road when he captured the WBA lightweight title on April 12, 1981, in Atlantic City, decisioning formerly undefeated Hilmer Kenty of the famed Kronk Gym in Detroit, Michigan.

2. VINNIE PAZIENZA

The "Pazmanian Devil," who has changed his legal handle name to "Vinny Paz," brought big-time boxing to Rhode Island in the early 1980s. He won all twelve of his contests in his home state and fought the majority of his contests in nearby New Jersey and Connecticut. Vinnie won the IBF lightweight title on June 7, 1987, in Providence, Rhode Island, winning a "hometown"—or at least debatable—decision over Greg Haugen. Pazienza moved up in weight later in his career. In March 2002, he lost a twelve-round decision to Eric Lucas for the World Boxing Council (WBC) super middleweight crown.

3. SVEN OTTKE

Germany's IBF super middleweight champion Sven Ottke has proved to be a worthy champion, making sixteen title defenses against some decent opposition. However, there have also been some controversial decisions against American contenders Charles Brewer and Thomas Tate. To his credit, Ottke defeated both boxers in rematches. Ottke has fought thirty-one of his thirty-two bouts in his native Germany, boxing in front of sold-out crowds of partisan well-wishers.

4. VIRGIL HILL

North Dakota's only professional sports franchise, Virgil "Quick Silver" Hill, hails from the city of Williston. He achieved star status by winning a silver medal at the 1984 Olympics in Los Angeles. As a professional, Hill has been a light heavyweight and cruiserweight champion. Hill has fought in several locations in his home state, including Minot, Fargo, and Bismarck.

5. TONY LOPEZ

Tony "The Tiger" Lopez's skills led him to become Sacramento's latest celebrated boxer, winning three world championships before finally hanging up his gloves in 1999. The Tiger filled Sacramento's Arco Arena several times, fighting in eight world title fights before the hometown fans. Lopez fought and won his first eighteen fights in Sacramento. Lopez's title-winning effort against Rocky Lockridge in Sacramento was named *The Ring* magazine's 1988 "Fight of the Year." All in all, Lopez fought in Sacramento forty times, winning thirty-seven bouts.

6. MATT VANDA

Known as "The Predator" to his legion of fans in East St. Paul, Minnesota, the heavily tattooed boxer is trained by former world title contender Brian Brunette and his brother, Tommy Brunette. "Vandamania" is gaining momentum in the one-time boxing hotbed of St. Paul. Although Minnesota no longer has a boxing commission of its own, big-time boxing is back in the Twin Cities. Vanda is currently 28–0 and hopes to fight for a world title in the near future. Boxing promoter (and former boxing great) Sugar Ray Leonard was in attendance at a Vanda bout in 2002, exploring the possibility of getting the Minnesota native some television exposure.

7. JOEY GAMACHE

Maine's first world titleholder, Gamache excited local boxing fans with his fast hands and flashy persona. Gamache's early career unfolded in Maine and overseas in France. Joey's two world titles were won in front of his fans in Maine, and several of his bouts aired on national television. Gamache won thirty fights in his home state. He retired in 2000 with a record of 55–4 after suffering a brutal knockout at the hands of Arturo Gatti,

Mike Fitzgerald

Heavily tattooed Matt "The Predator" Vanda is immensely popular in his native Minnesota and hopes to take his success nationwide.

who outweighed Gamache by nearly twenty pounds at fight time.

8.   THOMAS HEARNS

Thomas "The Hitman" Hearns fought fifteen of his first sixteen bouts in his native Michigan on his way to becoming a top contender. Hearns, who was also billed as "The Motor City Cobra," claimed his first title on August 2, 1980, by knocking out Pipino Cuevas in the second round at the Joe Louis Arena in Detroit to win the WBA welterweight title. Tommy fought another fifteen times in the Wolverine state in his illustrious career, winning titles in five different weight divisions.

9. KATSUYA ONIZUKA

The former WBA junior bantamweight champion, Katsuya Onizuka fought all twenty-four of his bouts in Japan, twenty-three of them in the capital city of Tokyo. He boxed out of the famed Kyoei Gym in Tokyo and fought most of his matches at the legendary Japanese fight arena Korakuen Hall. Onizuka won his world title on April 10, 1992, via a controversial decision over Thailand's Thanomsak Sithbaobay. Onizuka went on to make five title defenses, all at home, before losing his title and suffering a detached retina. Onizuka became very popular with the media and often called the fights at ringside for Japanese television.

10. KENNY KEENE

One of most popular athletes to hail from the state of Idaho, Kenny Keene won the lightly regarded International Boxing Association (IBA) cruiserweight championship. He hails from Emmett, Idaho, and is billed as the "Emmett Eliminator." Keene retired in 1999 with a record of 47–3 but returned to the ring in 2002. Keene has fought approximately forty bouts in "The Potato State" and has lost there only once. He has fought in his hometown of Emmett, Worley, and the capital city of Boise.

Debut Debacles

Most fighters with potential are matched against easy opponents right out of the gate to build their confidence and pad their record. Usually, these prospects face tomato cans in their opening bout. Then they gradually face tougher competition to see if they have what it takes to become a world-class fighter and even a champion.

It may surprise you to know that many world champions did not follow this traditional path. Either they were not considered prospects or had to come up the hard way. In fact, several failed to win their pro debut, including some boxers who ended up enshrined in the International Boxing Hall of Fame in Canastota, New York. They include:

1. **HENRY ARMSTRONG**

Henry Armstrong, known as "Homicide Hank," perennially ranks as one of the top fighters of all time. He captured the world featherweight, lightweight, and welterweight titles in his illustrious career. Even more remarkably, he held all three titles at the same time in 1938. Fearless and relentless, Armstrong overwhelmed opponents with his windmill style of attack. But he did not start off with a bang. On July 27, 1931, a fighter named Al Iovino stopped Armstrong in the third round in North Braddock, Pennsylvania. In fact, Armstrong lost three of his first four fights. But he later went on an incredible streak of twenty-seven straight knockout wins.

2. BENNY LEONARD

Benny Leonard, known as the "Ghetto Wizard," is considered by boxing experts to be one of the greatest, if not the greatest, lightweight in the history of boxing. He won the world championship in 1917 and held it until 1923. He had more than two hundred bouts in his spectacular career. Leonard turned pro at the age of fifteen in his home state of New York. In his debut, one Mickey Finnegan kayoed him in the third round. Few spectators probably realized that the losing fifteen-year-old kid would go on to become one of the sport's all-time greats.

3. ALEXIS ARGUELLO

Alexis Arguello, "The Explosive Thin Man," wreaked havoc in the featherweight, super featherweight, and lightweight divisions for much of the 1970s and early 1980s. He won world titles in all three divisions and later became the first boxer from Nicaragua inducted into the International Boxing Hall of Fame. But in his hometown of Managua, Nicaragua, on August 1, 1968, Arguello lost his pro debut at age sixteen against a fighter named Cachorro Amaya. Amaya stopped Arguello in the very first round. Though he began his career with a record of 2–2, Arguello retired with an impressive record of eighty wins and only eight losses.

4. MIGUEL CANTO

The diminutive flyweight Miguel Canto was a sight to behold. Nicknamed "El Maestro" for his brilliant boxing ability, Canto captured a world title and defended it an incredible fourteen times. He possessed great defensive skills, impressive stamina, and superb speed. But he had a less-than-stellar entry into the professional ranks. On February 5, 1969, Canto lost his pro debut in his birthplace of Merida, Mexico. A fighter named Raul Hernandez stopped him in the third round. Canto also lost his third fight by technical knockout. But this great little man mastered the artistry of boxing and was inducted into the International Boxing Hall of Fame in 1998.

5. BILLY CONN

Billy Conn, "The Pittsburgh Kid," was one of the greatest light heavyweight fighters of all time and a classic boxer. In 1941, he gave up his light heavyweight title to fight for the greatest prize in professional sports—the world heavyweight championship—against the great Joe Louis. Though he gave up thirty pounds to the "Brown Bomber," Conn boxed his way to the lead through twelve rounds. Then, in the thirteenth round, Conn ignored the advice of his corner and went for the knockout. Louis caught him with a devastating right hand that kayoed the overconfident Conn. Conn also lost his pro debut as a lightweight by dropping a four-round decision to one Dick Woodard in Fairmont, West Virginia. No one ever heard from Dick Woodard again, but Billy Conn boxed his way into the Hall of Fame.

6. BERNARD HOPKINS

Bernard "The Executioner" Hopkins shocked many in the boxing world by dismantling favored Felix "Tito"

Trinidad to unify the world middleweight championship on September 29, 2001. In his next bout, he defeated Carl Daniels to set the record with fifteen successive defenses of his middleweight crown. Hopkins has not lost a fight since 1993, when he dropped a twelve-round decision loss to the great Roy Jones Jr. In fact, Hopkins has lost only two fights his entire career. His only other loss occurred in his pro debut. On October 11, 1988, Hopkins lost a four-round decision to one Clinton Woods in Atlantic City, New Jersey. He fought then as a light heavyweight. After the bout, he wisely campaigned in lower weight classes—and is still adding to his credentials as an all-time middleweight great.

7. PIPINO CUEVAS

Pipino Cuevas ruled the welterweight division in the late 1970s with a pulverizing left hook. The popular Mexican champion defended his world title eleven times, ten by knockout. His domination of the division ended abruptly when he ran into the right hand of Thomas "The Hitman" Hearns, an all-time great. Cuevas turned pro at the young age of fourteen. His inexperience showed in his pro debut in Mexico City on November 14, 1971. Al Castro stopped the teenager in the second round. Cuevas struggled to a 7–5 log as he gained experience. But once he gained that experience, he went on a kayo tear.

8. MANUEL ORTIZ

Manuel Ortiz compiled ninety-six wins in the bantamweight division and had two title reigns in the 1940s. In his first reign as 118-pound king, he defended his title fifteen times. In a career that spanned 127 bouts, he was stopped only one time. His lengthy title reigns earned him induction into the International Boxing Hall of Fame in 1996.

But Ortiz lost his pro debut on February 25, 1938—though his loss was understandable. In his very first fight for pay, he faced top-ten contender Benny Goldberg, who decisioned him over four rounds. Ortiz would get revenge against Goldberg when Ortiz outpointed his old foe in November 1943 to retain his world bantamweight crown. The pair actually faced each other four times, each winning two.

9. MIKE WEAVER

Mike Weaver was called "Hercules" on account of his muscular physique. But it was his left hook that lifted him from mediocrity to the world heavyweight title. In 1980, Weaver faced undefeated "Big" John Tate for the WBA world title. Entering the fifteenth and final round, Tate was ahead on all three judges' scorecards. But with about forty-five seconds left in the bout, Weaver landed his vaunted left hook, and Tate fell face-first to the canvas. A most unlikely heavyweight champion was born. Weaver began his pro career with two losses to the same fighter, Howard Smith. On September 14, 1972, Smith stopped Weaver in the third round. A month later, Smith decisioned Weaver over five rounds. But Smith never became world heavyweight champion, and Weaver did.

10. JAMES "BONECRUSHER" SMITH

James "Bonecrusher" Smith won the world heavyweight championship when he upset champion "Terrible" Tim Witherspoon in the opening round, dropping him three times. Though he lost his belt to Mike Tyson in his next fight, Smith defeated other name fighters in his career, including kayos over former champions Frank Bruno and Mike Weaver. Smith did not fare well in his November 5, 1981, pro debut against vaunted amateur and pro prospect James Broad, who stopped Smith in the fourth round. Smith would rebound to win his next fourteen fights until losing to champion Larry Holmes in his first bid for a world title.

Ring Weirdness

Unquestionably, the sport of boxing has had its share of bizarre occurrences in and out of the ring. The following is a list of ten such occurrences that would hold their own in any "News of the Weird" column.

1. THE BITE

Biting in boxing is nothing new. There have been numerous reported instances of boxers engaging in this dirty tactic. But Mike Tyson took it to another level in June 1997 in his rematch with Evander Holyfield. Holyfield appeared to be getting the better of Tyson heading into the third round, much as he had in their previous encounter in 1996. Increasingly frustrated, Tyson actually came on in the third round landing some good body shots. But Holyfield kept firing back, and Tyson was cut over his eyes. During a clinch, Tyson literally bit a chunk out of Holyfield's ear. Referee Mills Lane deducted two points from Tyson and allowed the fight to continue. Amazingly, Tyson took a second bite, leaving Lane no choice but to disqualify Tyson for his egregious actions. The biting earned Tyson a one-year suspension by the Nevada State Athletic Commission.

2. FAN MAN

The second bout between then-world heavyweight champion Riddick Bowe and Evander Holyfield in November 1993 will be remembered for its nonstop action over twelve rounds. It will also be remembered for the actions of one James "Fan Man" Miller. That's because in the seventh round, Miller paraglided into the ring, landing near Bowe's corner. The bizarre scene delayed the fight for twenty-one minutes. Referee Mills Lane commented later in his autobiography, *Let's Get It On*: "The only redeeming thing about 'Fan Man's' unexpected entrance was that the sonofabitch landed in Bowe's corner." Bowe's cornermen proceeded to pummel "Fan Man" with several blows before security intervened.

3. THE CRYING GAME

Oliver "The Atomic Bull" McCall had captured the world heavyweight championship with a stunning upset of Lennox Lewis in 1994. Three years later, the two squared off again for the heavyweight crown in February 1997. In the meantime, McCall had lost his title to Frank Bruno and battled problems with the law and drugs. Unfortunately, McCall's personal demons engulfed him in his return bout with Lewis. For the first few rounds, Lewis kept McCall at bay with his superior jab and reach. Early in the bout, McCall turned his back and walked away from Lewis. At the end of the third round, McCall did not return to his corner but walked around the ring in a daze. His bizarre behavior peaked in the fifth round when he began weeping visibly in the ring. Referee Mills Lane had no choice but to stop the bout as the crying McCall refused to defend himself.

4. **BRIBERY DURING THE BOUT?**

In February 1993, heavyweight contender and former Olympic gold medalist Ray Mercer was on the verge of a million-dollar payday against then-undefeated champion and former Olympic teammate Riddick Bowe. All that stood in his way was journeyman Jesse Ferguson, who was viewed as nothing more than a tune-up for Mercer. However, on February 6, Ferguson took the fight to Mercer. HBO commentators noticed that in the bout, Mercer spoke repeatedly to Ferguson during several clinches. The commentators said they never heard such talking between opponents in a boxing ring. Ferguson alleged that Mercer began offering him a bribe to throw the fight in the third round. According to Ferguson, Mercer said: "Man, I don't got it tonight. I'll give you a hundred thousand dollars to go down." An HBO tape was less than conclusive but captured comments from Mercer such as "That's your cut, man" and "I'll give it to you tomorrow." Mercer vigorously denied such allegations. However, New York prosecutors brought bribery charges against Mercer. After a two-week trial, a jury acquitted Mercer after five hours of deliberation on March 29, 1994. However, Mercer lost his chance to face Bowe in the ring.

5. **LOW BLOWS**

Andrew "The Foul Pole" Golota had all the physical tools to become heavyweight champion. He was tall and strong and possessed a powerful left jab. Mentally, it was a different story. In July 1996, the undefeated Golota squared off against former world heavyweight champion Riddick Bowe in Madison Square Garden. The fight was a brutal affair with both fighters landing hard shots in several rounds. However, Golota clearly hurt Bowe more and was winning the fight on all three scorecards heading into the seventh round. Golota's only problem was that he kept throwing low blows. The referee had already deducted several points from him when, inexplicably, Golota battered Bowe in the groin with another clear low blow, which led to his disqualification. After the disqualification was announced, one of Bowe's cornermen attacked Golota and all hell broke loose in the crowd. It took more than half an hour for security to restore order.

6. SUCKER PUNCH

Traditionally, boxers embrace each other after the completion of their bout. Even fighters with little or no respect for their opponent will touch gloves or show some sign of mutual respect. Super middleweight James "The Harlem Hammer" Butler did no such thing after his second fight with Richard "The Alien" Grant on November 23, 2001. Grant had used his awkward style and slick movement to confound Butler and capture a ten-round decision. Butler was extremely frustrated with the fight and his performance. After the bout, Grant went over to shake hands. Butler unloaded a gloveless right-hand bomb on Grant's jaw. Grant collapsed to the canvas, coughing up blood. He later required surgery to fix his mouth. Butler faced assault charges and an indefinite suspension from the New York State Athletic Commission.

7. "NO MAS"

The legendary Roberto "Hands of Stone" Duran was one of the fiercest competitors in the history of boxing.

He was the epitome of machismo, which is why his actions in New Orleans in November 1979 were mystifying even to his staunchest supporters. Duran squared off against Sugar Ray Leonard, a man whom he had defeated via close decision the previous year in a bout called "The Brawl in Montreal." Duran had handed Leonard his first defeat as a pro. In the rematch, Leonard boxed smartly, refusing to become embroiled in another brawl. He began to frustrate and even taunt the proud Duran. In the eighth round, Duran dropped his hands in disgust and yelled, "No mas," which is Spanish for "no more." Duran later claimed he was suffering from stomach pains from losing too much weight too quickly. Whatever the reason, Duran's actions constituted a serious blotch on a nearly spotless career.

8. MAMA WILL KNOCK YOU OUT

In 1989, Tony Wilson squared off against undefeated Steve McCarthy at the Guildhall in Southampton, England. In the third round, McCarthy knocked Wilson down. Later, McCarthy pinned Wilson against the ropes. Apparently, Wilson's mother, Minna, took exception. She ran up to the ring and started beating McCarthy with her stiletto shoe. McCarthy left the ring and had to have four stitches. When order was restored, the referee ordered McCarthy to return to the ring. When McCarthy refused, the referee declared Wilson the winner by third-round technical knockout. "I don't know what happened to me," said Minna, who indicated she was upset by racial slurs hurled at her son. "I am really sorry." For his part, Tony Wilson barred his mother from attending any of his future fights.

9. THE KICKING HEAVYWEIGHT

In 1991, rising star Riddick Bowe entered the ring against Elijah Tillery, a former sparring partner for Mike

Tyson. It was expected to be another routine win for Bowe on his path to the heavyweight crown. Bowe came out in the first round and dominated, dropping Tillery to the canvas. At the end of the round, Tillery mouthed off at Bowe, who jabbed back at his opponent. Then the real melee began as Tillery kicked Bowe three times, prompting Rock Newman, Bowe's loquacious and combative manager, to grab Tillery by the neck and try to pull him over the rope. Bowe threw a roundhouse right for good measure. Tillery tumbled out of the ring, nearly carrying Bowe with him. The referee disqualified Tillery for unsportsmanlike conduct. Tillery told reporters at a press conference: "I did it in the heat of combat. I got a fighting spirit, man."

10. THE COLLAPSING RING

In October 1998, two journeyman heavyweights—with emphasis on heavy—squared off at the Nashville Fairgrounds in Nashville, Tennessee. Ed "The Giant" White, who stood 6'6" and weighed nearly 280 pounds, faced Kenneth Bentley, who himself damaged the scales at about 245 pounds. Neither fighter possessed a good record. White had a record of about 6–4, while Bentley sported an abysmal ledger of 8–73–1. The fight turned into a hugging affair as Bentley grabbed his larger opponent and hung on. In the second round, White lunged awkwardly into Bentley, who was already languishing on the ropes. The result will linger in the minds of all three hundred people at this club show— the entire ring collapsed. Amazingly, the staff responded quickly and reinstalled a dislodged ring post. The fight continued with White winning via technical knockout in the third round.

Bibliography

Books

Anderson, Dave. *In this Corner: Boxing's Greatest Trainers Talk about Their Art*. New York: William Morrow & Company, 1991.

Ashe, Arthur R. Jr. *A Hard Road to Glory: The African American Athlete in Boxing*. New York: Harper-Collins, 1993.

Bak, Richard. *Joe Louis: The Great Black Hope*. New York: De Capo Press, 1998.

Collins, Nigel. *Boxing Babylon: Behind the Shadowy World of the Prize Ring*. New York: Citadel Press, 1990.

Early, Gerald (ed.). *The Muhammad Ali Reader*. Hopewell, New Jersey: The Ecco Press, 1998.

Fleischer, Nat, and Sam Andre. *An Illustrated History of Boxing* (sixth ed.). New York: Citadel Press, 2001.

Goldstein, Alan. *A Fistful of Sugar: The Sugar Ray Leonard Story*. New York: Coward, McCann & Geoghegan, 1981.

Hauser, Thomas. *Muhammad Ali: His Life and Times*. New York: Simon & Schuster, 1991.

Heller, Peter. *In This Corner. . . !* New York: Simon & Schuster, 1973.

Hietala, Thomas R. *The Fight of the Century: Jack Johnson, Joe Louis and the Struggle for Racial Equality.* Armonk, New York: M.E. Sharpe, Inc., 2002.

Holmes, Larry (with Phil Berger). *Against the Odds.* New York: St. Martin's Press, 1998.

Johnston, Alexander. *Ten and Out! The Complete Story of the Prize Ring in America* (fourth ed.). New York: Ives Washburn, 1943.

Kent, Graehme. *Boxing's Strangest Fights: Incredible but True Encounters from over 250 Years of Boxing History.* London: Robson, 2001.

Kram, Mark. *Ghosts of Manila: The Fateful Blood Feud Between Muhammad Ali and Joe Frazier.* New York: HarperCollins, 2001.

Lane, Mills (with Jedwin Smith). *Let's Get It On.* New York: Crown Publishers, Inc., 1998.

Lipsyte, Robert, and Peter Levine. *Idols of the Game: A Sporting History of the American Century.* Atlanta, Georgia: Turner Publishing, Inc., 1995.

Morrison, Ian. *Boxing: The Records.* Enfield, Middlesex: Guiness Books, 1986.

Newfield, Jack. *Only in America: The Life and Crimes of Don King.* New York: William Morrow and Company, 1995.

Oates, Joyce Carol. *On Boxing* (second ed.). Hopwell, New Jersey: The Ecco Press, 1995.

Odd, Gilbert. *The Encyclopedia of Boxing.* Edison, New Jersey: Book Sales, 1989.

Roberts, James B., and Alexander Skutt. *The Boxing Register* (third ed.). Ithaca, New York: McBrooks Press, 2002.

Robinson, Sugar Ray (with Dave Anderson). *Sugar Ray*. New York: Viking Press, 1970.

Sammons, Jeffrey. *Beyond the Ring: The Role of Boxing in American Society*. Champaign: University of Illinois Press, 1988.

Shavers, Earnie (with Mike Fitzgerald and Marshall Terrill). *Welcome to the Big Time*. Champaign, Illinois: Sports Publishing L.L.C., 2002.

Sugar, Bert, and John Grasso. *505 Boxing Questions Your Friends Can't Answer*. New York: Walker and Company, 1982.

Sugar, Bert et al. *The Great Fights: A Pictorial History of Boxing's Greatest Bouts*. New York: The Rutledge Press, 1981.

Sugar, Bert et al. *100 Years of Boxing*. New York: Galley Press, 1982.

Sullivan, Russell. *Rocky Marciano: The Rock of His Times*. Champaign: University of Illinois Press, 2002.

Periodicals

Boxing Digest (formerly *International Boxing Digest*)

The Cyber Boxing Zone (http://www.cyberboxingzone.com)

Fightnews.com (http://www.fightnews.com)

The Ring

The Ring Almanac (annual publication)

The Boxing Record Book, Fight Fax, Inc. (yearly publication)

Index

Ali, Laila, **129–30**, 141, 217

Ali, Muhammad, 5, **16–17**, **23**, 49, 60–61, 87–88, 93, 95–96, 117, 121–24, 128–30, 135, 137, 154,, **157–58**, 160, 171, **178**, 183, 187–88, 190–94, 197–99, 206, 215, 218, 227 (*See also* Cassius Clay)

Allen, Laurie, 171

Alvarez, Rosendo, 8, 126, 235

Alzado, Lyle, **135**

Amaya, Cachorra, 246

Ambers, Lou, 214

Anderson, Dave, 205

Anderson, Steve, 147

Andre the Giant, **160**

Arbachakov, Yuri, 51

Arcel, Ray, **214**

Archibald, Joey, 93

Arguello, Alexis, 13, 75, 185, **246**

Armstrong, Henry, 12, **36**, **41**, **202**, **245–46** (*See also* Jackson, Henry)

Atkins, Ken, **95**, **97**

Atlas, Teddy, 25

Austin, Steve, 158

Avelar, Antonio, 233

Ayala, Mike, **126–27**

Ayala, Tony (Jr.), **126–27**

Ayala, Tony (Sr.), 126

Baer, Buddy, **126**

Baer, Max, **23**, **42–43**, **126**, 157, **177**, 181

Bailey, John, **153**

Baillargeon, Rosario, 106

Barkley, Iran, 187

Barry, Jimmy, **7**

Basilio, Carmen, 5, 163

Bassa, Fidel, 52

Becerra, Antonio, 12

Bedwell, Roy, 65, **67–68**

Beery, Wallace, 182

Belanger, Charley, 4

Belcher, Jem, 2

Ben Guesmia, Muhammed, 73

Benitez, Wilfred, **44–45**, 212, **228**, 232

Bennett, Michael, **90–91**

Bentley, Ken, **65**, 256

Bentt, Michael, **188**

Benvenuti, Nino, **20**

Berbick, Trevor, 46

Bernal, Gabriel, 50

Berg, Jackie ("Kid"), 45, 85, **210–11**

Bivins, Jimmy, 41, **56–57**, **238**

Black, Julian, 225

Blackburn, Jack, **225**

Blanco, Rodolfo, 9

Bodzianowski, Craig, 177

Bogart, Humphrey, 181

Bonavena, Oscar, 89, 95

Bond, Ward, 182

Booker, Rydell, 70

Borboa, Julio Cesar, 234

Botha, Francois, 84

Boudaini, Laurent, 73

Bowe, Riddick, **18–19**, 61, 84, 252–56

Braddock, James, **23**, 42, 126

Bradley, Shazzon, **136**

Brady, Peter, 77

Bramble, Livingstone, 120, 230

Braxton, Dwight, 87, 124 (a.k.a. Dwight Muhammad Qawi)

Breland, Mark, 145

Brennan, Bill, 40

Brewer, Charles, 38, 241

Brewster, Lamon, 188
Bridges, Jeff, 180
Briggs, Shannon, 65,
  67, **79**, 140
Briscoe, Bennie, 118,
  233
Britton, Jack, 210
Broad, James, 250
Broughton, Jack, **2**
Brouhton's Rules, 2
Brown, Aaron Lister
  ("The Dixie Kid"),
  113, 210
Brown, Derrick, **189**
Brown, Drew ("Bun-
  dini"), 187, 197
Brown, Joe, 227
Brown, Marselles, **139**,
  150
Bruno, Frank, 217, 250,
  252
Brusso, Noah, 204 (See
  also Burns, Tommy)
Buchanan, Ken, 85
Buck, Timothy, 1
Buffer, Michael, 200
Bugner, Joe, 71, 89,
  176
Burge, Bella, **219–20**
Burge, Dick, 219
Burley, Charley, **55**,
  239
Burns, Tommy, **204**,
  223 (See Brusso,
  Noah)
Burton, Tony, **186**
Butler, James, 254
Buttrick, Barbara, **218**
Byun, Jung-Il, **52**
Byrd, Chris, **119–20**,
  131
Byrd, Joe, **119–20**, 131
Byrd, Robert, **189**
Byrd, Tracy, **131**, 132

Camacho, Hector (Jr.),
  121, 230
Camacho, Hector (Sr.)-
  ("Macho"), **121**,
  229–30
Camel, Marvin, 207
Campos, Newton, 76

Cane, Dante, 63
Cannon, Jimmy, 98,
  221
Canto, Miguel, 51, **247**
Canzoneri, Tony, **45**
Carbajal, Michael, **19–
  20**, 51
Cardona, Prudencio,
  233
Cardona, Ricardo, **233**
Carlson, Sue, 218
Carnera, Primo, 23, 42–
  43, 126, 136, **157**,
  180, 214
Carney, Jem, 7
Carpentier, Georges, 4,
  167
Carrasco, Pedro, 46
Carter, Jimmy, 192
Casanova, Baby, 226
Castillo, Eliecer, 188
Castillo, Freddy, 233
Castro, Al, 248
Celestine, Jerry, 87
Cervantes, Antonio
  ("Kid Pambele"), 13,
  44, **212**, 228, **232**
Chambers, John Gra-
  ham, 1
Chang, Jung-Koo, 50
Charles, Ezzard, 57, 62,
  80, 92, 216, 225,
  237, 239
Chavez, Julio Cesar, **31**,
  229–30
Chip, George, 3
Chitalada, Sot, **50**, 51
Chocolate, Kid, 45,
  203, **210**, 211
Chow, Loi, 219
Choynski, Joe, 109,
  209
Churchill, Winston, 98
Chuvalo, George, 95,
  193
Clark, Lamar, 186
Classen, Marilyn, 104
Classen, Willie, **103–4**
Clay, Cassius, 5, **22**, 87,
  88, 95–96, 135, 166,
  191 (See also Mu-
  hammad Ali)

Clay-Bey, Lawrence,
  137
Clayton, Zack, 188, **225**
Cobb, Randall ("Tex"),
  144, 175
Coe, David Allan, 173
Coetzee, Gerrie, 28, 185
Cole, Alfred, 152, **188**
Collins, Billy Jr., **110**
Collins, John, 145
Conn, Billy, 26, **29–30**,
  42, 108, 196, **247**
Cook, Eddie, 234
Cooney, Gerry, 25, 167,
  172, 186, 199
Cooper, Andre, **208**
Cooper, Bert, 163
Cooper, Henry, 95
Coopman, Jean-Pierre,
  60, 193
Corbett, James J.
  ("Gentleman Jim"),
  3, 14, 54, 182, 195,
  197, 224
Corn, Jonathan, 70
Corretjer, Millie, 171
Corro, Hugo, 233
Costner, George, **207**
Cox, Luis, 235
Cream, Arnold, 166,
  202 (See also Walcott,
  Jersey Joe)
Cribb, Tom, **2**, 222
Croot, Walter, 7
Cruz, Carlos, 46
Cruz, Roberto, 217
Cuevas, Pipino, **45**,
  243, **248**
Cummings, Floyd
  ("Jumbo"), **89**
Curry, Bruce, **127**
Curry, Donald, **127**
Czyz, Bobby, 161

D'Amato, Cus, 88
Daniels, Carl, 248
Daniels, Robert, 67
Daniels, Terry, **63–64**
Dauthuille, Laurent,
  27–28
Davey, Chuck, **163**

DeJesus, Esteban, **17–18**, **229**
De La Hoya, Oscar, 125, 150, **171**, 228–230
DeLeon, Carlos ("Sugar"), 65, **206–7**
Del Valle, Lou, 131
Dempsey, Jack ("the Manassa Mauler"), 4, 11–12, **24**, **40**, 55, 93, 124, 154, **155–56**, 167, 198, 214
Dempsey, Jack ("the Nonpareil"), 3
De Niro, Robert, 181
Denkin, Marty, **189**
Denny, Cleveland, 106
De Wit, Willie, **162**
DiBiase, Mike, 88, **158–59**
Dixie Kid, **113**, **210**, 224 (*See also* Brown, Aaron Lister)
Dixon, George, 45, 48, 221, **222–23**
Dixon, Robert, **173**
Dixon, Willie, **172**
Donavan, Art, 169
Donavan, Arthur, **168–69**
Donavan, Mike, 168
Dore, Art, 152
Dorsey, Troy, **144**
Douglas, Bill, **118**, 142
Douglas, James ("Buster"), **21**, 61, **118**, **141–42**, 185
Doyle, Jimmy, **100–101**
Drayton, Buster, 50
Drazenovich, Chuck, **136**
DuBois, W.E.B., 53
Dundee, Angelo, 32, 216
Dundee, Chris, **216**
Dundee, Johnny, 45
Dundee, Joe, 123, 216
Dundee, Vince, 123
Dunn, Richard, 61
Dunphy, Don, **215**

Dupas, Ralph, 208
Duran, Irichelle, **131**
Duran, Roberto, **17–18**, 50, **85**, 106, 110, 121, 131, **183**, 199, 206–7, 214, 229, 254–55
Durelle, Yvon, 41
Durham, Richard, 178
Duva, Lou, 59, 76
Duvall, Robert, 178
Duvergal, Alfredo, **32–33**
Dylan, Bob, 101

Eastwood, Clint, 185
Eaton, Aileen, **217**
Ellis, Jimmy, 5, 39, 89, 128, 192
Elorde, Flash, 227
Emanuel, Armand, **164**
Erne, Frank, 45, 223
Escalera, Alfredo, 15, **75**
Esch, Eric ("Butterbean"), 68, 122, **149–50**, 238
Escobar, Sixto, 93, **226**
Espada, Angel, 45
Espadas, Guty (Jr.), **119**, **162**
Espadas, Guty (Sr.), **119**
Etienne, Clifford, **89**, **137**
Evangelista, Alfredo, 63
Everett, Tyrone, **15**, **75**

Famechon, Johnny, 166
Felstein, Bob, 95
Feour, Royce, 78
Fenech, Jeff, **49**, 128
Ferguson, Jesse, **61–62**, 253
Ferns, James ("Rube"), 82, 224
Fernandez, Perico, 49
Fields, Sedreck, 136
Fields, Tye, **140**, 148
Figg, James, **1**
Finkel, Shelly, 76

Finnegan, Mickey, 246
Firpo, Luis Angel, 40
Fitzgerald, Mike, 68
Fitzsimmons, Robert (Bob), **2–3**, 14, 70, 175, 181, 195
Fleischer, Nat, 156
Flores, Pedro, 14
Flowers, Tiger, **76–77**, **236–37**
Flynn, Errol, 182
Foreman, Freeda, 129–130
Foreman, George, **23**, **25**, **29**, 71, **79**, 85, 88, 129–130, 176, **177**, 188–91, 198–99
Forrest, Vernon, 207, **238**
Foster, Bob, 26, **93**, 128
Fox, Billy, 40
Foxx, Jamie, 187
Frank, Scott, **59–60**
Frawley Law, 57
Frazier, Joe, **5**, **16**, 25, 62–64, 71, 89, 93, 95, **117–18**, 128–130, 141, **171**,172, **186**, 187, 190, 199, 215
Frazier, Marvis, **117–18**
Frazier, Richard, **94**
Frazier-Lyde, Jacqui, **129–30**, **141**
Frias, Art, 120
Fullmer, Gene, 4, 40
Futch, Eddie, 16, 55, **214–15**

Gaines, Joseph, 223 (*See also* Gans, Joe)
Galaxy, Khaokor, **125**
Galaxy, Khaosai, **13**, **36**, 125, **204**
Galento, Tony, 83
Galindez, Victor, **108–9**, 118
Gamache, Joey, **242–43**
Gannon, Rocky, **152**
Gans, Joe, 221, **223**, 225

Garcia, Jimmy, **105–6**, 116
Gardner, George, 3
Garfield, John, 180
Garr, Sam, **239**
Gastineau, Mark, **134**
Gatti, Arturo, 242
Gavilan, Kid, 163, **204**, 207, **211** (*See also* Gonzalez, Gerardo)
Gaye, Marvin, 170
Gennaro, Frankie, 214
George III, 2
Giardiello, Joey, 56
Gibbons, Mike, **124**
Gibbons, Tommy, **92–93**, **124**
Gibbs, Fredia, **141**
Gilbert, James, **189**
Gimbel, Bernard, 77
Gimenez, Carlos, 232
Gogarty, Deidre, 217
Goldberg, Benny, 249
Goldman, Herbert, 80
Goldstein, Alan, 106
Goldstein, Ruby, 18, 99, **168**
Golota, Andrew, **84**, 253–54
Gomez, Wilfredo, **37–38**, **227–28**
Gonzalez, David, **104–5**
Gonzalez, Gerardo, 204, 211 (*See also* Gavilan, Kid)
Gonzalez, Humberto, **19–20**
Goodman, Charley, 3
Goosen, Joe, 125
Gordy, Berry, 172
Graham, Billy, 204
Graham, Herol, 43
Grant, Michael, **139**, 140
Grant, Richard, 254
Graziano, Rocky, **17**, 40, 163, 182, 185
Greb, Harry, 12, 56, 77, **83**, 214, 237
Greene, Richard, **116**
Grey, Harold, **234–35**
Grier, Pam, 178

Griffin, Montell, 11
Griffith, Emile, **18**, **20**, **98–99**, 168, 212, 217
Grim, Joe, **69–70**
Gushiken, Yoko, **14**
Gutenko, John, 211 (*See also* Williams, Kid)

Haggard, Merle, 173
Hagler, Marvelous Marvin, 104, 167, 206, 208
Haley, Leroy, 127
Hall, Jake, 68
Halpern, Mitch, **115–16**, 235
Hanna, Tom, 170
Harada, Masahiko "Fighting", 166, 171
Harmon, Derrick, 70
Harris, Clarence, 208
Harris, George, **66**
Harris, Maurice, 67
Harrison, Audley, **163–64**
Hart, Gaetan, 106
Hart, Garnet, **208**
Hatton, Ricky, 153
Haugen, Greg, 241
Haynes, Ricky, 145
Hazzard, Larry (Sr.), **188**
Hearns, Thomas, **31–32**, 45, 97, 167, 206, **243**, 248
Hefton, Brad, 144
Heller, Peter, 30, 82
Herman, Pete, 74
Hernandez, Arturo, 78
Hernandez, Gabriel, **115**
Hernandez, Raul, 247
Hide, Herbie, 188
Highsmith, Alonzo, **134–35**
Hill, Sam, **94**
Hill, Virgil, **241**
Hinckley, John, 199
Hines, Frankie, 65
Hinton, Jemal, **9**
Hiranaka, Akinobu, 111

Hiranaka, Nobutoshi, **110–11**
Hitz, Bobby, **176–77**
Holbaek, Dennis, 153
Holcomb, Jeff, 66
Holden, Tony, 199
Holly, James, **66**
Holmes, Larry, 12, **25–26**, 28, **36**, 40, 59, 63, 118, 124, 167, **172**, 192, 199, 214, **238**, 250
Holmes, Lindell, 208
Holyfield, Evander, 9–10, **18–19**, **22**, 26, **75–76**, 84, **85**, 114, 116, 118–20, 167, 251–52
Hong, Soo-Hwan, 233
Hope, Maurice, 45, 228
Hopkins, Bernard, 229, **247–48**
Hopson, Ed, 121
Huber, Hans, 5
Hudson, David, 102
Hughes, Troy, **147**
Hunsaker, Tunney, **95–96**

Inoki, Antonio, 148, **157–58**
Ioka, Hiroki, 14, **37**, **52**
Iovina, Al, 246
Izon, David, 34

Jack, Beau, 204, **237**
Jackson, Henry, 202
Jackson, Melody, 202
Jackson, John, 3
Jackson, John ("Big"), 144
Jackson, Julian, **43**
Jackson, Peter, **54**, 221, **224**
Jacob, Thierry, 121
Jacobs, Joe, 196–97
Jacobs, Mike, 215
Jeanette, Joe, 53–54, **57–58**, **168**
Jeffries, James J. (Jim), 3, **14**, **165**, 195, 223
Jimmerson, Art, 173

Jirov, Vassili, 90
Johansson, Ingemar, 18, 23–24, 47, 131
Johansson, Maria, 131
Johnson, Fred, 222
Johnson, George ("Scrap Iron"), 71
Johnson, Jack, 14, 54–55, 58, 70, 76, 107–8, 154–55, 165, 167–68, 175, 181, 223
Johnson, Marvin, 118
Johnson, Stan, 68
Johnston, Alexander, 57
Jones, Anthony, 230
Jones, Bobby, 237
Jones, Ed ("Too Tall"), 133–34
Jones, George Khalid, 102–3
Jones, James Earl, 178
Jones, Junior, 234
Jones, Roy Jr., 11, 94, 138–39, 150, 170–71, 196, 229, 248
Joppy, William, 229
Jordan, Don, 212
Julio, Jorge Elicier, 234

Kaczmarek, Jim, 73
Kallen, Jackie, 219
Kameda, Akio, 8
Kates, Richie, 87
Keach, Stacey, 180
Keene, Kenny, 244
Kellerman, Max, 102
Kennedy, John, 120
Kennedy, Leon Isaac, 180
Kenty, Hilmer, 240
Ketchel, Stanley, 112, 165
Kiatwanchai, Napa, 52
Kilrain, Jake, 197
Kim, Duk Koo, 99, 116
Kim, Ji-Won, 8
Kim, Sang-Hyun, 49
Kim, Yong Kang, 50
King, Don, 76, 152, 199, 203, 218

Kittikasem, Muangchai, 50, 51
Kitterman, Ernie, 145–46
Klitschko, Vitali, 123, 143, 161
Klitschko, Wladimir, 123, 140, 143, 153, 161
Koch, Cody, 153
Kristofferson, Kris, 178
Kugler, Phyllis, 218

Laguna, Ismael, 19, 227
LaMotta, Jake, 4, 27–28, 40, 181, 185
Lampley, Jim, 29, 79
Landry, Tom, 133
Lane, Mills, 167, 199, 251–253
Langford, Sam, 53, 54, 55, 58, 225
LaPaglia, Lenny, 145
LaPorte, Juan, 37–38, 84, 108, 228
Lavigne, George ("Kid"), 211, 224
Lederman, Harold, 75, 79
LeDoux, Scott, 159–60
Lee, Cowboy Rocky, 156
Leija, Jesse James, 125
Leno, Jay, 149
Leonard, Benny, 168, 214, 246
Leonard, Sugar Ray, 31–32, 85, 106, 118, 121, 167, 199, 206, 207, 242, 254–55
Letterlough, Julian, 89–90
Levinksy, Battling, 40
Lewis, Harry, 210
Lewis, John Henry, 224–25
Lewis, Lennox, 26, 75–76, 85, 139, 161, 252
Lewis, Panama, 110
Lewis, Ted ("Kid"), 3–4, 210
Liebling, A.J., 205

Limon, Rafael ("Bazooka"), 121, 229
Lindecker, Scott, 150
Liston, Sonny, 22, 86–87, 95, 121, 166, 188, 191, 198
Lizeviche, Antonio, 109
Lockridge, Rocky, 37, 228, 242
Londos, Jim, 157
Lopez, Alfonzo, 119
Lopez, Danny, 12, 127
Lopez, Eddie ("the Animal"), 185–86
Lopez, Ricardo, 8, 35–36, 37
Lopez, Tony, 241–42
Lopez, Yaqui, 87
Loughran, Tommy, 164
Louis, Joe, 29–30, 35, 42, 63, 79–80, 83, 92, 108, 126, 154, 156, 168–69, 196, 213–14, 221, 224–25, 238, 247
Lovell, Aberto Santiago, 184
Lovell, Pedro, 184
Loy, Myrna, 177
Lucas, Eric, 138, 241
Luttrell, Clarence, 155–56
Lyle, Ron, 25, 88–89, 128

Macalos, Tacy, 51
Machen, Eddie, 71
Maddalone, Vinny, 152
Magramo, Ronnie, 126
Mahone, Ed, 153
Maldonado, Oscar, 234
Malloy, Dallas, 219 (See also McLeery, Jennifer)
Mamby, Saoul, 229
Mancini, Lenny, 119–20
Mancini, Ray, 99, 116, 119–20
Mandell, Sammy, 225
Manley, Joe, 8
Marcano, Alfredo, 46
Marchegiano, Rocco

Francis, 203 (*See also* Marciano, Rocky)
Marciano, Rocky, 3, **6**, 26, **30**, 41, **42**, **203**, 237 (*See also* Marchegiano, Rocco Francis)
Markes, Jack, 4
Markson, Harry, **215**
Marino, Tony, 226
Marquis of Queensberry, 1, 83, 155, 182
Marsh, Terry, **8**
Marshall, Lloyd, 41, **239**
Martel, Belle, **220**
Martin, Bob, 78
Martin, Christy, **151–52**, **217–18**
Martin, Leotis, 87
Maskaev, Oleg, 26, 34
Mathis, Buster, 89
Maxim, Joey, 57, 114, 168
Mayorga, Ricardo, 238
Mayweather, Floyd Jr., **118**
Mayweather, Floyd Sr., **118**
Mayweather, Roger, 118
McCall, Oliver, 252–53
McCarthy, Steve, 255
McCauliffe, Jack, **7**
McClellan, Gerald, 70
McCline, Jameel, 139, **140**
McCoy, Al, **3**
McCoy, Charles ("Kid"), 82, **113**, **209–10**
McCrory, Milton, **127–28**
McCrory, Steve, **127–28**
McFarland, Packey, **13**, **57**
McGovern, Terry, **45**
McGregor, Margaret, **219**
McGuigan, Barry, 37
McLaglen, Victor, **175**, 181
McLarnin, Jimmy, 45, 168, **213–14**

McLeery, Jennifer, **219**
McMillan, Colin, 233
McNeeley, Peter, **121–22**
McNeeley, Tom, **121–22**
McQueen, Steve, 176, 182
McTigue, Mike, **76**
McVey, Sam, 53–54, **58**
Mendoza, Bebis, **235**
Mendoza, Daniel, **3**
Mendoza, Luis, **234**
Mercante, Arthur (Jr.), 102
Mercer, Ray, 61, 253
Merchant, Larry, 21, 29, 79
Meredith, Burgess, 179
Michaels, Shawn, 158
Michel, Louis, 76
Mihari, Tidashi, 50
Miller, Dusty, 13, 57
Miller, James ("Fan Man"), 252
Miller, Reggie, 135
Milligan, Henry, **164**
Mills, Freddie, 114
Miske, Billy, 56
Molineaux, Algernon, 222
Molineaux, Tom, 2, **222**, 224
Monroe, Willie, 118
Monzon, Carlos, **108**, 233
Moon, Sung-Kil, 125
Moore, Archie, **41**, 47, 55, 57, **88**, 131, **158–59**, 184, **202** (*See also* Wright, Archibald)
Moore, J'Marie, **131–32**
Moore, Davey (junior middleweight) **50**, **110**
Moore, Davey (featherweight), **101**, 206, 217
Moorer, Michael, **25**, **29**
Morales, Erik, 119, 162
Moran, Frank, 167

Morel, Eric, **231**
Morrison, Tommy, 25, 29, **150**, **184**, 185, 188
Mosley, Shane, **207**, 238
Motta, Dick, 27
Muangsurin, Saensak, **48–49**
Muhammad, Eddie Mustafa, 87, 124
Muhammad, Matthew Saad, 118
Muniz, Alicia, 108
Murphy, Lee Roy, **32**
Mutti, Chisanda, **32**

Nakajima, Shigeo, 51
Nelson, Andrea, **152**
Nelson, Azumah, 38, 49, 105–6, 125
Nelson, Battling, 57, 223
Nevitt, Mike, **145–46**
Newfield, Jack, 199
Newman, Paul, 182
Newman, Rock, 256
Nielson, Brigitte, 134
Norfolk, Kid (a.k.a. William Ward), **56**
Norris, Orlin, 84
Norris, Terry, 43, 105, 127
Norton, Ken, **17**, 25, 36, 39, 63, 128, **137**, 167, 176, **178**, 184, 189, 192, 215, 238
Norton, Ken (Jr.), 137
Norwood, Freddie, 234
Nunn, Michael, 127, 187

Oates, Joyce Carol, 112
O'Brien, Jack ("Philadelphia"), 225
Odd, Gilbert, **215**
O'Dowd, Mike, 3, 214
O'Grady, Pat, 240
O'Grady, Sean, **240**
Oguma, Shoji, 51
O'Halloran, Jack, **176**
O'Hara, Maureen, 181

Ohba, Masao, **109**
Olin, Bob, 224
Olivares, Ruben, 171
Oliveira, Ray, **208**
Olivo, Joey, 14, 37
Olson, Carl ("Bobo"), 4, 40–41, 114, 132
Olson, Eliza, **132**
Oma, Lee, **62**
Onizuka, Katsuya, **244**
Oquendo, Fres, 34
Ortiz, Carlos, **19, 227**
Ortiz, Manuel, **248–49**
Ottke, Sven, **38**, 115, **241**
Owen, Johnny, **103**

Pacheco, Irene, **235**
Pacquaio, Manny, 234
Page, Greg, 66, 184
Page, James, 239
Palacio, Ruben, **233–34**
Palomino, Carlos, 44, **162**, 228
Palmer, Tom, 45
Panica, John F., 214 (*See also* Wilson, Johnny)
Papke, Billy, **112–13**, 165
Papp, Lazlo, **7, 56**, 227
Paret, Benny, **18, 98–99**, 168, 208, **212**
Park, Chan-Hee, **51**
Pastrano, Willie, 227
Patterson, Floyd, 5, **18, 23–24, 47**, 48, 60, 87, **120–21**, 128, 131, 191
Patterson, Tracy Harris, **120–121**
Payne, Tyrone, 90
Pazienza, Vinnie, **240–241**
Pedroza, Eusebio, **37, 83–84**
Pendleton, Freddie, 125
Penelton, Donnie, **70–72**
Pep, Willie, 41, **166**, 205
Percy, Earl, 222

Perez, Raul, 234
Perrin, Jimmy, **93**
Pesci, Joe, 181
Petelo, Zolani, 37
Pharr, Kerry, 97
Piccirillo, Michele, 122
Pintor, Lupe, 38, **78, 103**
Porpaoin, Chana, **125–26**
Porpaoin, Songkram, **125–26**
P'ouha, Samson, 84
Powell, Charley, **135**
Poyner, Heather, 219
Pritchard, James, 144
Pryor, Aaron, **12–13**, 106, 212, 232

Qawi, Dwight Muhammad (a.k.a. Dwight Braxton), 87
Quarry, Mike, **128**
Quarry, Jerry, 63, 71, **128**
Quinn, Anthony, 180

Rabanales, Victor, 52
Racine, Ralph, 106
Rademacher, Pete, 48, **60**
Rahman, Hasim, **26**, 34, 85
Rahway State Prison, 87
Ramirez, Jose Luis, **76**, 121, 229–30
Ramon, Mario, 168
Ramos, Mando, **46**
Ramos, Ultiminio ("Sugar"), **80–81, 101, 206**, 217, 227
Randolph, Leo, 233
Rangel, Alfred, 144
Reagan, Nancy, 198
Reagan, Ronald, 198
Reid, David, **32–33**, 94, 229
Resto, Luis, 110
Rickard, George ("Tex"), 4
Richmond, Bill, 2, **221–22**

Rijker, Lucia, 132
Robertson, Floyd, **80–81**
Robinson, Jason, 70–71
Robinson, Sugar Ray, **4–5**, 27, **40**, 55, **100–101, 113–14**, 168, **201–2**, 204, **205–6**, 207–8 (*See also* Smith, Walker)
Rocap, Billy, 74
Rockne, Knute, 136
Rodgers, Mike, **173–74**
Rodriguez, Luis, 208, 217
Roosevelt, Theodore, 98
Roper, Jack, **63**
Rosario, Edwin, 121, 229, **230–31**
Rose, Lionel, **171**
Rosenbloom, Maxie, 109
Rosier, Kevin, **147–48**
Ross, Barney, 36, 214
Ross, Diana, 172
Roth, William, 79
Roufus, Rick, **147**
Routis, Andre, **85**
Roxborough, John, 225
Ruelas, Gabriel, **105–6**, 116, **124–25**
Ruelas, Rafael, **124–25**
Ruffin, Jimmy, 93
Ruiz, John, 85, 196
Runyon, Damon, 23
Ryan, Jim, 82
Ryan, Tommy, 82

Saddler, Sandy, **41**, 173
Saksuree, Sakda, 13
Salamone, Melissa, **131**, 132
Salas, Joe, 85
Salazar, Carlos, 235
Saldivar, Vincente, 81, 206
Sammartino, Bruno, 160
Sammons, Jeffrey, 99
Sanchez, Salvador, **12, 108**, 228

Sanders, Corrie, 143, 161
Santiago, Manuel, **71**
Saxton, Kassan, 91
Scalzo, Petey, 94
Schmeling, Max, 42–43, 169, 196–97, **213**, 214
Schroeder, Ricky, 182
Schulberg, Bud, 196
Schutte, William, 82
Scott, James, **87**
Scottland, Beethaeven, **102–3**
Scypion, Wilford, **103–4**
Seales, Ray, **207–8**
Serrano, Samuel, 46
Shain, Eva, **218**
Shain, Frank, 218
Shannon, Robert, 9
Sharkey, Jack, 40, 196–97, 213, **214**
Shavers, Earnie, **39**, 62, 67, 89, 119, 128, **159**, **176**, 192, **203**, 218
Sheppard, Arnold ("Kid"), **70**
Shibata, Kuniaki, 46
Shingaki, Satoshi, 49
Shufford, Charles, **188**
Siki, Battling, 56
Silvani, Al, **185**
Simpson, Angelo, **71**, **73**
Sinatra, Frank, 185
Singleton, Benji, **73**
Sitbangprachan, Pichit, **9**
Skelly, Jack, 48, 222
Slack, Jack, 2
Smith, Amos ("Mysterious Billy"), **82**, 224
Smith, Charley ("Tombstone"), 208
Smith, Ed ("Gunboat"), 40
Smith, Howard, 249
Smith, James ("Bonecrusher"), 46, **162**, **249–50**

Smith, Walker, 201–2
Smith, Will, 187
Snipes, Renaldo, 59
South Woods State Prison, 87
Spearman, Jose, 70
Spears, James, **139–40**
Spinks, Cory, **122**
Spinks, Leon, **49**, 68, **122–24**, 137, 186, 193–94
Spinks, Michael, **12**, **25–26**, 36, **123–24**, 172
Sproul, Andre, **154–55**, 167
Stallone, Sylvester, 176, 179, 183
Stander, Ron, 59, **62–63**
Starling, Marlon, 118
Steele, Richard, 31, **166–67**
Stevenson, George, 2
Strahan, Michael, 134
Stribling, Young ("William Lawrence), **109**, **236**
Strickland, Reggie, **70**, 71
Studd, ("Big") John, 159
Sugar, Bert, 80
Sulaiman, Jose, 76
Sullivan, John L., 54, 182, 197
Summitt, Pat, 141
Sutherland, Murray, 152

Takechi, Seiji, **115**
Tapia, Johnny, 234
Tate, John, **28**, 186, 249
Tate, Thomas, 241
Taylor, Bud, 225
Taylor, Estelle, 198
Taylor, George, 2
Taylor, Jermain, 94
Taylor, Meldrick, **31**
Terrell, Ernie, **172**, 188, 191–92
Terrell, Jean, 172

Thomas, Pinklon, 67
Thomburifam, Mai, 52
Thunder, Jimmy, 188
Tiberi, Dave, **78–79**
Tiger, Dick, 93, 227
Tillery, Elijah, 255–56
Tilman, Henry, 163
Tillis, James, **177–78**
Tinley, Mike, 208
Toney, James, **78–79**, **187**, 219
Torres, Battling, 217
Torres, Jose, **227**
Trafton, George, **136**
Trimiar, Lady Tyger, **218**
Trinidad, Felix, **228–29**, 247–48
Trump, Donald, 79
Tryon Reform School, 88
Tua, David, 26, **33–34**, 119–20
Tucker, Tony, 46, 186
Tunney, Gene, **11–12**, **24**, 83, 93, 124, 198
Turpin, Randy, 4, **113–14**
Tyson, Mike, 12, **21–22**, **46**, **84**, 85, **88**, 89, 116, 118, 121, 124, 137, 142, **158**, 164, 167, 177, 197, 217, 227, 249, 251–52, 255–56

Ulrich, Thomas, 70
Ursua, Armado, 51

Valdez, Rodrigo, **232–33**
Vanda, Matt, **242–43**
Vasquez, Wilfredo, 125
Velasquez, Miguel, 49
Velasquez, Rico, 105
Verners, Terry, 135
Villa, Pancho, 214
Villaflor, Ben, **46**
Voight, Jon, 182
Vorasingh, Netrnoi, **45–46**
Vorapin, Ratanapol, **37**

Walcott, Joe ("the Barbados Demon"), **109**, 113, 210–11, 223, **224**

Walcott, Jersey Joe, 6, **30**, 42, **79–80**, **92**, 156, **166**, 168, 181, **202**, 225, 237 (*See also* Cream, Arnold)

Walker, Jimmy, 197

Walker, Mickey, **77**, 164

Wallace, Nunc, 222

Walker, Sidney, 237 (*See also* Jack, Beau)

Wallau, Alex, 78

Wangila, Robert, **104–5**

Ward, Stan, **184–85**

Ward, Vonda, **140–41**

Warring, James, 67, **143–44**

Waters, Muddy, 172

Wayne, John, 181

Weathers, Carl, 183

Weaver, Mike, **28**, 177, 185, **249**, 250

Wepner, Chuck, 59, **160**, 183

Whitaker, Pernell, **76**

White, Ed, 256

Wilder, James, **68**

Willard, Jess, 40, 223

Williams, Bobby, 168

Williams, Eugenia, 75

Williams, Holman, 41

Williams, Ike, 163, 204, 207, **237**

Williams, Keith, 147

Williams, Kid, 74, **211–12**

Williams, Mike, **185**

Williamson, DaVarryl, **163**

Wills, Damien, **189**

Wills, Harry, 53–54, **55**, 58

Wilson, Johnny, **214**

Wilson, Tony, 255

Winfrey, Oprah, 177

Wipperman, Dick, **95**

Wisniewski, Jim, **68**

Witherspoon, Carla (Shakurah), **132**

Witherspoon, Tim, 132, 162, 185, 249

Wofford, Danny, **67**

Wolfgramm, Paea, 148

Womack, Rickey, **9–10**, **114–15**

Woodard, Dick, 247

Woods, Clinton, 248

Worth, Teddy, **71**

Wright, Archibald, 202

(*See also* Moore, Archie)

Wynn, Milton, **173**

Yakushiji, Yasuei, 52

Yanger, Benny, 77

Yates, Brian, **67**

Young, Bobby Joe, 13

Young, Jimmy, 25

Yuh, Myung-Woo, **14**, **37**

Yost, John, **151**

Young, Bobby Joe, 13

Yuh, Myung-Woo, **37**, 52

Yum, Dong-Kyun, 37–38

Zale, Tony, **17**, 182, 214

Zanon, Lorenzo, **63**

Zapata, Hilario, **51–52**

Zarate, Carlos, **78**

Zbysko, Larry, **159–60**

Zivic, Fritzie, 11, 36, 40, **82–83**

Zukauskas, Joseph Paul, 214 (*See also* Sharkey, Jack)

Zwick, Phil, **94**

About the Authors

David L. Hudson Jr. is an author, attorney, and feature writer for Fightnews.com. His boxing articles have appeared in *Boxing Digest* and *The Cyber Boxing Zone*. Hudson is a licensed boxing judge and a member of the Tennessee Boxing Advisory Board. He lives in Smyrna, Tennessee, with his wife, Carla.

Mike H. Fitzgerald Jr. is a graduate of Loras College in Dubuque, Iowa. A former boxer and current judge, matchmaker, and promoter in Wisconsin, Fitzgerald ghostwrote books on 1970s heavyweights Ken Norton and Earnie Shavers and title-contending amputee Craig "The Gator" Bodzianowski. Fitzgerald currently resides in Janesville, Wisconsin, with his wife, Debra, and their son, Ross.